# SOME PROBLEMS OF INDIAN LITERATURE

# SOME PROBLEMS
## OF
# INDIAN LITERATURE

by

**M. WINTERNITZ, M.A., Ph.D.**

GYAN

*Published by*

Gyan Publishing House
5, Ansari Road
Daryaganj, New Delhi-110002
Phone: 011-47034999, 9811692060
E-mail: books@gyanbooks.com

*Distribution Network*
gyanbooks.com
India, USA, Canada, UK, Australia, France



ISBN : 978-81-212-2599-1 (PB)
First Published, 1925

2nd Impression 2021

*Printed at:* Gyan Press, Delhi.



**Some Problems of Indian Literature**
Author: M. Winternitz

# SOME PROBLEMS OF INDIAN LITERATURE

CALCUTTA UNIVERSITY READERSHIP LECTURES, 1923

By

M. WINTERNITZ, M.A., Ph.D.

CALCUTTA UNIVERSITY PRESS

1925

# CONTENTS


| | Pages |
|---|---|
| The Age of the Veda ... ... ... | 1–20 |
| Asiatic Literature in Ancient India ... ... | 21–40 |
| Ancient Indian Ballad Poetry ... ... | 41–58 |
| Indian Literature and World-Literature ... | 59–81 |
| Kautiliya Arthasastra ... ... ... | 82–109 |
| Bhāsa ... ... ... ... | 110–130 |

# THE AGE OF THE VEDA[1]

First of all I have to thank the authorities of this University for honouring me with an invitation to lecture to their students and graduates. For one who has made the study of Indian literature and culture his life's work for the last forty years, it is naturally the fulfilment of a long-cherished desire to come to India, to see with his bodily eye the land and the people with whom he has for many years been familiar in the spirit. That this fulfilment has come to me at last, for this I cannot be thankful enough to the poet Rabindranath Tagore who has extended to me his kind invitation to lecture at *Visvabharati*—this ingenious and courageous attempt at realising a poet's dream. It has been a great delight to me to lecture to and to work with the students of this new University at Santiniketan and it is a new pleasure to me to be able to-day to open a course of lectures for the students of this her much older sister University.

When I first came to Calcutta I was asked by an Indian lady, how I came to be interested in Indian literature. She seemed to think it strange and somewhat extraordinary that a European should take an interest in the literature of India. And it may indeed seem strange to some of you that I as a non-Indian should speak to you about your own literature. But there is nothing wonderful at all in the interest we take in the West in the literature of India. For the history of the literary

[1] Readership Lecture delivered at the Calcutta University in August, 1923.

treasures of ancient India appears to us only as part and parcel of the history of man. In this sense Indian literature is as much ours as it is yours. The ideas and thoughts of great men belong to mankind, and not to any one country or nation only. To us, therefore, the history of Indian literature is nothing but one great chapter, one of the most brilliant and most important chapters in the history of the human mind.

It is also one of the most difficult chapters,—difficult on account of the lack of absolutely certain historical data. The chronology of Indian literature is shrouded in darkness, so much so, that it is impossible to give any certain dates for its oldest periods. We have to be satisfied, if we can ascertain with a greater or lesser degree of *probability* the *limits* within which the oldest and most important literary works may be dated.

The first and the greatest and at the same time the most difficult of all the difficult problems in the history of Indian thought, is that of *the age of the Veda.*

The Veda stands at the head of Indian literature, not only on account of its age, but also because no one who has not gained an insight into the Vedic literature can ever understand the intellectual and spiritual life and the culture of India. This is a matter of course for Brahmanic India, as Brahmanism is based on the Veda. But Buddhism also and all other Indian creeds, can never be fully understood by one who knows nothing of the Veda. For in some way or other all Indian religions are linked to the thoughts contained in the *Upanishads,* the latest productions of Vedic literature which presuppose the Brāhmaṇas as these again presuppose the hymns and prayers of the *Vedic Saṃhitās,* above all the hymns of the *Ṛgveda,* which is doubtless the oldest Indian and most probably also the oldest Indo-European literary monument. How important it would be to know the exact date of such a monument! And yet we have to confess that up to now the views of the best scholars differ with regard to the age of the Veda not by centuries, but by millenniums, that some scholars lay down the year 1000 B.C. as the lowest limit for the Ṛgvedic hymns, while others would go back to a period between 3000 and 2500 B.C. When the views of eminent scholars differ from each other so very much it is not sufficient to state the different opinions, but it becomes necessary to enter into the details of the question and to examine the arguments on which these scholars base their divergent views; to give a full account of the present state of the question and to show how far it is possible to arrive at any more or less definite conclusions, and how far we must resign ourselves to confessing that we do not know anything more at present.

When Indian literature became first known in the West, people were inclined to ascribe a hoary age to every literary work hailing from India. They used to look upon India as something like the cradle of mankind, or at least of human civilization. The better, however, we became acquainted with Indian literature, the more this view had to be given up, and scholars became cautious and suspicious and a tendency arose, to make everything as late as possible. Indians, on the other hand, have always had a sentimental inclination, to consider their most important works of literature, above all the Veda, as immensely old. According to the orthodox Brahmanical view, indeed, the Veda has been created at the beginning of the world and is no human work at all. The historian has to abandon this view, and he has to free himself from all preconceived opinions and inclinations. I, for my part, do not understand why some Western scholars are so anxious to make the hymns of the Ṛgveda and the civilisation which is reflected in them so very much later than Babylonian and

Egyptian culture. Nor do I understand why Indians should think that it adds anything to, or detracts anything from, the *value* of the most beautiful hymns of the Ṛgveda or the deepest passages of the Upanishads according as they are believed to be a thousand or five hundred years older or later.

The first scholarly attempt at fixing the age of the Veda was made by Max Müller in his "History of Ancient Sanskrit Literature" published in 1859. Starting from the few definite facts of Indian chronology we possess, the invasion of Alexander and the rise of Buddhism, he went on concluding as follows. Buddhism is nothing but a reaction against Brahmanism and it presupposes the existence of the entire Veda (Saṃhitās, Brāhmaṇas, Āraṇyakas and Upanishads). The whole of this literature, therefore, must be pre-Buddhistic, that is, it must have arisen before 500 B.C. The Vedānga and Sūtra literature probably arose simultaneously with the origin and early spread of Buddhism. These Sūtra works which Max Müller placed in the period from 600 to 200 B.C., presuppose the Brāhmaṇas. For the Brāhmaṇas of which there are older and newer ones and which contain long genealogical lists of teachers a period of at least 200 years must be assumed. Hence he dated the origin of the Brāhmaṇa literature from 800 to 600 B.C. The Brāhmaṇas again presuppose in their turn the Vedic Saṃhitās. At least 200 years were necessary for the compilation of all these collections of songs and prayers. Therefore, Max Müller argued, we may take the period of about 1000 to 800 B.C., as the time when the Vedic Saṃhitās were arranged. But this arrangement of the Saṃhitās which were already considered as sacred sacrificial poetry and sanctioned prayer books, must have been preceded by a period when the prayers and songs contained in them were composed as popular or religious poetry. This period,

Max Müller concluded, must lie before 1000 B.C. And as he had assumed 200 years for what he called the "Brāhmaṇa period" and again 200 years for his "Mantra period," he also assumed 200 years for the growth of this poetry and so arrived at the date 1200 to 1000 B.C., as the beginning of Vedic poetry.

Now it was a mere guess on the part of Max Müller when he gave the dates 600 to 200 B.C. for the origin of the Sūtra literature. And the assumption of 200 years for each of the periods in the development of the Veda was quite arbitrary. Instead of 200 years he might just as well have said 300 or 400 years. Max Müller himself did not wish to say more than that our Ṛgveda-Saṃhitā must have been completed *at least* about 1000 B.C. That he meant no more by his tentative chronology than fixing a *minimum* date for the origin of the Vedic hymns, he stated clearly in his Gifford Lectures on Physical Religion (1890) where he says that we cannot hope to find the date, when the earliest Vedic hymns *began* to be composed. He says here: "Whether the Vedic hymns were composed 1000 or 1500 or 2000 or 3000 years B.C., no power on earth will ever determine."[1]

And yet, strange to say, although the foundation on which Max Müller's calculations were based, was so purely hypothetical and arbitrary, it had become a habit among scholars for a long time, to speak of 1200 to 1000 B.C., as the date of the Ṛgveda, which Max Müller was said to have established. And to many people it appeared as something like a heresy when (in the year 1899) the Indian scholar Bal Gangadhar Tilak and the German scholar H. Jacobi (simultaneously though independently from each other, tried to prove a much higher age of the Veda. Both these scholars started from astronomical

[1] Max Müller—Physical Religion, Gifford Lectures, new edition, 1898, p. 91.

calculations. They both came (though on different ways) to the conclusion that in the time of the Brāhmaṇas the Kṛttikas (Pleiades which were the first of the 27 Nakshatras coincided with the vernal equinox, but that in Vedic texts we also find traces of an older calendar in which the vernal equinox fell in Mṛgaśiras (Orion). Now certain astronomical calculations lead to the result that about 2500 B. C. the vernal equinox fell in the Pleiades and about 4500 in the Orion. Tilak concluded from this that some Vedic texts go back to the year 6000 B.C., while Jacobi placed the beginning of Vedic culture, that is, of the epoch to which the Vedic hymns belong at about 4500 B. C., and he assumed that this epoch extended from about 4500 to 2500 B. C., and he would ascribe the Ṛgveda to the end of this period.

In this view Jacobi was confirmed by another astronomical consideration. We find in the Gṛhyasūtras the description of an ancient Hindu marriage custom according to which the bride and bridegroom, after arriving in their new home had to sit silently on a bull's hide, until the stars became visible, whereupon the bridegroom pointed out to the bride the polar star, called *Dhruva*, 'the constant one' and said the Mantra 'be constant, prospering with me,' and she replied: 'Constant art thou, constant may I be in the house of my husband.' The name *Dhruva* and the whole ceremony prove that this polar star was considered to be unmovable and therefore a symbol of constancy, of conjugal fidelity. Such a name and such a custom can only have arisen at a time when a *bright* star was the polar star. A star, however, to which the name *Dhruva* could be applied, and which was bright enough to be pointed out at the marriage custom mentioned was near the Pole in the year 2780 B. C. To this time Jacobi would ascribe the origin of the name Dhruva and of the marriage custom of showing the 'constant' star to the bride. This custom is, however, not mentioned in the marriage hymn of the Ṛgveda. Jacobi, therefore, regards it as probable 'that the employment of the Dhruva in the wedding ritual belongs not to the time of the Ṛgveda but to the following period, and that, therefore, the Ṛgveda period of civilisation lies before the third millennium B.C.'

The arguments both of Tilak and of Jacobi have been severely criticised not only by Vedic scholars but also by such high authorities on Indian astronomy as Thibaut. The fact is that it is extremely difficult to be quite sure about the commencement of the year in different millenniums. The Śatapatha-Brāhmaṇa (12, 8, 2, 35) says: 'All seasons of the year are the first, all the middle ones and all the last.' And from early times the beginning of the year was reckoned in India sometimes with spring, sometimes with winter and sometimes with the monsoon. It has also been doubted whether the Indians in ancient times paid any attention to the equinoxes. Against Jacobi's argument taken from the Polar star and the Dhruva marriage rite it has been urged that the requirements of the ritual would be satisfied by any star of some magnitude which was appropriately polar." [1]

Lately B. V. Kamesvara Aiyar [2] has again tried by astronomical data about the Kṛttikās and about the beginning of the year to prove that the Brāhmaṇas belong to a period of approximately 2300 B.C. to 2000 B.C., which would lead us for the Ṛgveda to a period of about 4500 B.C., the date of B. G. Tilak.

It seems to me extremely difficult to follow all these astronomical arguments, and to build a chronological edifice on a foundation the solidity of which is at least subject to great doubts.

[1] Macdonell by and Keith, Vedic Index, I, p. 427.

[2] Quarterly Journal of the Mythic Society, 1922.

I, therefore, attach greater importance to the *historical arguments*. And on *historical* grounds the age of the Veda must, in my opinion, be placed nearer the date assumed by Jacobi and Tilak than to that adopted by Max Müller, Oldenberg, Macdonell and Keith. It seems to me impossible to account for the development of the Vedic literature from the earliest hymns of the Ṛgveda to the later Upanishads and for the historical and political changes—which must have taken place from the times of the Ṛgveda to the period of the Sūtra literature which immediately followed the Upanishads within the space of 600 or 700 years from 1200 to 600 or 500 B.C.

Let us remember what the *Veda* really is. The Veda is neither one single book like the *Koran* nor a complete collection of a certain number of books compiled at some particular time as the Hebrew '*Old Testament*' or the Christian '*New Testament*' or the Buddhist '*Tipiṭaka*.' But what we call Veda is a whole *great literature*;[1] this literature consist of three distinct classes of literary productions. The first class of works are collections of hymns, prayers, magic songs and formulas (Saṃhitās) which were handed down in schools of priestly singers from generation to generation by word of mouth. Only one Ṛgveda-Saṃhitā, two Atharvaveda Saṃhitās (the Śaunaka and the Paippalāda recensions), one Sāmaveda-Saṃhitā, four Saṃhitās of the Yayurveda and a fifth one only in fragments, have come down to us, but we know that many more Saṃhitās must have existed. The second class of works are the voluminous prose treatises, called *Brāhmaṇas*, containing chiefly discussions on the sacrifice, and the practical or mystical significance of the numerous rites and ceremonies connected with the great sacrifices. A great number of Brāhmaṇas, attached to each one of the

[1] That may rather be compared with the Old Testament together with New Testament and with the Talmud than with any one of these.

Saṃhitās, has been preserved. But again we know, that many more had existed. The third class of works are the 'Araṇyakas' and 'Upanishads,' texts containing secret doctrines both of ritual and philosophy, some of which are included in the Brāhmaṇas or attached to them, while others are handed down as independent texts.

Every text belonging to one of these three classes of literature is called 'Vedic' that is, belongs to the Vedas. And the whole 'Veda' or 'Vedic literature' presents itself as a long line of religious works—collections of hymns and songs, prayer books, treatises on sacrifices and theosophical tracts—which represent a unity only in so far as they form the basis of the Brahmanical religious system. They are all considered as '*Sacred* books' which are not human work, but divine creation or revelation. But what is called 'Scripture' in other religions is termed '*Śruti*' or "Hearing" in Brahmanism, because the sacred texts were not written and read, but only recited and *heard*. This also is of chronological significance. It is clear, that a *written* literature can develop in a shorter time than one that is only handed down by word of mouth, when each single text requires generations of teachers and disciples in order to be preserved at all.

Now there cannot be the least doubt, that of all the works that belonged to the Veda, *the Hymns of the Ṛgveda* are the oldest, this is proved beyond doubt by the *language* of the hymns which represents a much older form of Indian speech than the language of the Brāhmaṇas. It is proved also by their versification. On the one hand, *Vedic metrics* seems to be separated from that of classical Sanskrit poetry almost by a gulf, as we find in the Vedic hymns metres of which there is no trace in later Sanskrit poetry, while on the other hand, numerous metres of classical Sanskrit poetry have nothing corresponding in the Ṛgveda. And some Vedic metres which are found in later poetry also appear there with a rhythm that is far more strictly fixed than in the Ṛgveda.

Again another proof of antiquity of the Vedic hymns is their *accentuation.* The Vedic accent is, like that of ancient Greek, of a musical nature, depending on the pitch of the voice; while in classical Sanskrit we only have a stress accent, depending on quantity. Only in the Veda the accent is marked, not in Sanskrit. Hence only the Vedic accent is of importance for Comparative Philology, while in the later language the accent has been shifted so that it can no longer be used for comparison with other Indo-European languages.

Again the *geographical, political, social and economic conditions*, as reflected in the hymns of Ṛgveda, point to a far higher antiquity than those described in the Brāhmaṇas and even in the Saṃhitās of the Yayurveda.

But the language which proves the high antiquity of the hymns, also proves that the Ṛgveda-Saṃhitā is not a uniform work, *of one time*, but consists of earlier and later strata of hymns. Other facts, too, show that the period in which these hymns were composed, must have extended over many centuries. The Ṛshis who not only in the Anukramaṇis, but already in the Brāhmaṇas are erroneously described as the 'seers' or authors of the hymns, are in these hymns themselves often referred to as sages of olden times. The authors of the hymns often speak of '*old* songs' or of 'songs composed in the *old* way,' thus indicating that this kind of poetry had been cultivated from times immemorial. And when we look at the great variety of the contents of the Ṛgveda —for we find in it not only hymns in praise of the gods, invocations and sacrificial songs, but also ballads and fragments of worldly poetry, philosophical hymns and magic songs,—we cannot help gaining the conviction that we have to see in this collection the *remnants of the oldest*

*Indian poetry in general*, that it contains only a small portion of a much more extensive (religious and secular) poetic literature, most of which seems to be irretrievably lost. As the bulk of the hymns are sacrificial chants, there can be no doubt that these form the nucleus of the whole collection, which was intended as a book of sacrificial songs and prayers. But the compilers, whether from some literary interest or from carelessness or ignorance, did not hesitate to include in it also profane poetry which, by language and metre, proved itself to be equally ancient and venerable as those sacrificial songs. But the greater part of this poetry was thought to be too profane to be included in the Ṛgveda-Saṃhitā.

And again when we look at the monumental work of M. Bloomfield, the 'Vedic Concordance' which is an index of every verse and line of the Veda, and at the same scholar's 'Ṛgveda Repetitions' (both published in the Harvard Oriental Series) in which no less than 5,000 of the 70,000 lines of the Ṛgveda are proved to be repetitions, we must conclude that at the time when the bulk of the hymns were composed there existed already a great number of verses which were considered as everybody's property that could be freely used by every poet as he liked. All this shows that the hymns collected in the Ṛgveda-Saṃhitā represent only the *last outcome*, the *final completion* of a literary activity that had been going on for a very long time. *Centuries must have passed between the composition of the earliest hymns and the completion of the Saṃhitā of the Ṛgveda.*

And yet it cannot be too strongly emphasised, that *even the latest parts* of the Ṛgveda are older than all the rest of Indian literature. This is proved by the fact that the Ṛgveda presupposes nothing of what we find in later Vedic and general Indian literature, while the whole of the later literature *presupposes* the Ṛgveda.

All the other Saṃhitās, though the Atharvaveda and the Yajurveda Saṃhitās contain much that is as old as the hymns, of the Ṛgveda, are yet as Saṃhitās later than that of the Ṛgveda. The Brāhmaṇas, Āranyakas and Upanishads, again, presuppose not only the hymns of the Ṛgveda, but also the prayers and formulas of the other Saṃhitās which are all considered as extremely old and sacred texts. In many cases these old hymns and prayers were no longer understood. Old myths and legends had fallen into oblivion and were told by the ritualists in their own way. One example for this is the legend of *Pūrūravas and Urvaśī* which is told in the Śatapatha-Brāhmaṇa. There the Ṛgvedic ballad containing the dialogue between Pūrūravas and Urvaśī is quoted. Yet the story of the Śatapatha-Brāhmaṇa is so far removed in time from the Ṛgveda, that it is not sufficient to elucidate the enigmatic verses of the Ṛgvedic ballad.

Another even more striking example of the distance between the hymns of the Ṛgveda and the Brāhmaṇas is the legend of *Śunaḥśepa* in the Aitareya-Brāhmaṇa. This is one of the gems of ancient Indian narrative literature, told in simple prose, mixed with verses. (This mixture of prose and verse had always been a favourite form of Indian literature.) Here the verses are of two kinds; Ṛgveda verses, some hymns of the Ṛgveda being included in the tale, and *Gāthas*, verses which both in language and in metre are entirely different from the Vedic verses and approach the epic. The legend itself is an important document for the history of Indian civilisation as it proves the occurrence of human sacrifices in very ancient times. It is also remarkable from a historical point of view. The story ends with the following sentences :

"This is the Ākhyāna of Śunaḥśepa which contains over a hundred Ṛg-verses and besides Gāthas. This legend is told by the Hotṛ priest to the king, after he has been sprinkled with holy water at the Rājasūya. Seated on a golden cushion he tells the story. Seated on a golden cushion the Adhvaryu priest gives the responses. Gold indeed signifies glory.

Thereby he causes his glory to increase. '*Om*' is the response to a Ṛg-verse, *tathā* ('yes') that to a *Gātha*, '*Om*' being divine, *tathā* human.[1] In this way he releases him from calamity and sin both by divine and by human word. Therefore a king who wishes to be victorious, though he be no sacrificer, may have the legend of Śunaḥśepa related to him; then not the least particle of sin will attach to him. He shall present a thousand cows to the narrator of the story, hundred cows to the priest who gives the responses, and besides to each of the two priests the golden cushion on which he has been sitting; moreover a silver chariot harnessed with mules should be given to the Hotṛ priest. Those, too, who are longing to have a son, shall have the legend recited to them, then they will certainly obtain a son."

This shows that the tale of Śunaḥśepa was a legend of time-honoured age already at the time when the Aitareya-Brāhmaṇa was compiled. Otherwise the recitation of the story could not have formed part of the ritual at the Rājasūya. The legend itself must be still older. It must be very old, as it refers to human sacrifices which in primeval times must have formed part of the Rājasūya, though neither in our Brāhmaṇa nor in the Śrautasūtras human sacrifices are ever mentioned in the ritual for the consecration of a king. And yet compared with Ṛgveda the legend of the Śunaḥśepa is modern. For the hymns which according to the Aitareya-Brāhmaṇa were seen by Śunaḥśepa have nothing to do with the legend, and several of the verses in which Śunaḥśepa is mentioned, cannot possibly have Śunaḥśepa as their author. This shows again, how far removed in time the hymns of the Ṛgveda are even from Brāhmaṇa legends of very respectable antiquity. Centuries must have passed between the completion of the Ṛgveda-Saṃhitā and the

[1] This clearly indicates that the Ṛig verses were considered as sacred while the Gāthas belonged to profane literature, when the Aitareya-Brāhmaṇa was composed.

compilation of the Brāhmaṇas, Āraṇyakas and Upanishads. Again, the Brāhmaṇas themselves with their numerous schools and branches of schools, with their endless genealogical lists of teachers, their numerous references to elder teachers require some centuries for their origin and growth. The Upanishads, too, belong to different periods. The Bṛhadāraṇyaka, Chāndogya, Taittirīya, Aitareya, Kaushītaki and Kena Upanishads which in style and language are not different from the Brāhmaṇas, form the oldest stratum of the Upanishad literature. A second stratum is formed by the Kāṭhaka, the Īśa, the Śvetāśvatara, the Muṇḍaka and the Mahā Nārāyaṇa-Upanishads, which by their metrical form differ from the Brāhmaṇas and contain nothing like the sacrificial mysticism of the Āraṇyakas. A third class of Upanishads, the Praśna, Māṇḍūkya and Maitrāyaṇīya Upanishads are again composed in prose but prove themselves by language, style and teaching as belonging to a still later period.

All these Upanishads again presuppose generations of teachers and a long tradition.

And yet during the whole time from the first beginnings to the last off-shoots of Vedic literature the Indo-Aryan people have only conquered the comparatively small area from the Indus to the Ganges. If it took such a long time for Aryan civilisation to spread only from the extreme North-West to the Eastern Ganges District, how many centuries must have been required not only for Vedic literature but at the same time also for Brahmanical culture, theology and even priestly supremacy to pervade the whole of Central and Southern India.

But inscriptions prove that in the 3rd century B.C. Southern India was already overrun by Aryan Indians, and Brahmanical civilisation prevailed in the south to such an extent that Vedic schools like those of Baudhāyana and Āpastamba arose there. It is not probable that immediately after the conquest the whole land should have been colonised and Brahmanised to such a degree, that Vedic schools could arise in the distant South. The conquest of Southern India by the Aryans must have taken several centuries before it became so complete, that important Vedic schools could arise there. We have to remember that the Deccan was not inhabited by primitive wild tribes, but by peoples who had a civilisation which very likely was in no way inferior to that of the Aryan invaders. In the times of the Ṛgveda the Aryans were still living within the comparatively small area of the extreme North-West of India and Eastern Afghanistan. From some of the hymns of the Ṛgveda we know that the Aryans already in those early times were divided into many tribes, and that some of these tribes lived in continuous warfare. Under these circumstances it is only natural that the Aryan conquest of the whole of India could proceed but very slowly and step by step.

Now the landmark which Max Müller once set up for the end of the Vedic period, the rise of Buddhism in the 5th century B. C. still exists. Buddha's teaching presupposes the existence of the whole Veda, including at least the six oldest Upanishads, probably also the second stratum of Upanishad literature. Only of the Maitrāyaṇīya-Upanishad it is certain that it is later than Buddha. But even before the rise of Buddhism there have been ascetic sects in India which rejected the authority of the Veda. One of these sects is that of the Jains. And it is now believed that Mahāvīra, the contemporary of Buddha, was not the founder, but only a reformer of the Jain sect, founded by Pārśva as early as 750 B.C.

Older than the grammarian Pāṇini is Yāska, the first commentator of the Ṛgveda known to us. In very early times already Indian scholars busied themselves with the explanations of difficult words in the Vedic hymns. Collections of words and meanings were compiled, the Nighaṇṭus or "glossaries." These form the basis for Yāska's Nirukta. Yāska, however, already quotes no less than seventeen predecessors whose opinions frequently contradict each other. Nay, one of the teachers quoted by Yāska went so far as to say that the whole Veda interpretation is worth nothing as the hymns are obscure, senseless, full of contradictions,—to which Yāska aptly replies that it is not the fault of the beam if the blind man does not see it. Yāska with his predecessors will not be very far from the time, when the sect of Pārsva and other Veda-rejecting ascetic sects arose.

If we ascribe the earliest hymns of the Ṛgveda to about 1200 B.C., as the scholars mentioned do, there remain only seven centuries for the development of the Vedic literature and for all the great political, social and economic changes which we have pointed out. It seems to me that both the political and the religious and literary history of India require at least twice as much time, to be rightly understood which means that the earliest hymns of the Ṛgveda must be nearer to 2000 B.C., than to 1200 B.C.

The question of the age of the Veda has of late again been discussed in connection with certain discoveries which have been made in 1907, by Hugo Winckler in Boghazköi in Asia Minor. Amongst the clay tablets found at Boghazköi there were also some documents concerning contracts concluded between the king of the *Hittites* (14th century B.C.) and the king of Mitani and as protectors of these contracts a number of Babylonian and native deities are invoked, and besides the gods of Mitani we also find the names :

(ilāni) mi-it-ra aś-śi-il (ilâni) u-ru-w-na-aś-śi-el (ilu) in-dar (ilâni) na-sa-a (t-ti-ia-a) n-na. These words have been read by Winckler and other scholars as referring to Mitra, Varuṇa, Indra and Nāsatyau. The historian Ed. Meyer saw in these names the names of Aryan gods, that is, he ascribed them to the period when Indians and Iranians formed as yet only one people. Oldenberg and Keith looked upon these names as those of an old Iranian people, closely related to the Vedic Indians. But as a matter of fact, the names Mitra, Varuṇa, Indra and Nāsatyau are only known as Vedic gods and we have no right to speak of them as 'Aryan' or 'Iranian.' If the names have been correctly read, we shall have to assume that Aryan Indians, perhaps only a band of warriors, had about 1400 B.C. by some chance come so far West as Mitani. But I do not think that this discovery proves much for the age of the Veda. For even if it can be proved that some of the gods whom we know from the Veda were invoked in Mitani about 1400, we can legitimately conclude that it is likely enough that at this time there were also hymns to these gods sung in the North-West of India, but it is impossible to say for how long a time such hymn poetry had been already known in that part of India. Thus I do not believe that the discovery of Boghazköi, provided that the readings of the tablets are correct, proves anything more than that Vedic culture is at least as old as the 15th century B.C.

The only serious objection against dating the earliest Vedic hymns so far back as 2000 or 2500 B.C. is the close relationship between the language of the old Persian cuneiform inscriptions and the Awesta. The date of the Awesta is itself not quite certain. But the inscriptions of the Persian kings are dated, and are not older than the 6th century B.C. Now the two languages, Old Persian and Old High Indian, are so closely related, that it is not difficult to translate the old Persian inscriptions right into the language of the Veda.

But this can only be a warning against going too far back in our date. The two languages cannot well be separated by many thousands of years. On the other hand, languages differ very much as to how long old forms of speech may be kept up, and there is a great difference between the languages of one family as to the time they want for differentiation. Lithuanian is one of those Indo-European languages which are nearest related to the ancient Indo-Iranian. But yet it is not an old language and its literature is of quite recent growth. And we do not know for how long a time the Vedic people of North-West India and the Iranian people may have lived in close neighbourhood even after their separation.

But one thing is quite certain. It is absolutely impossible to use geological evidence as Abinas Chandra Das does in his book 'Ṛig-Vedic India' (published by the University of Calcutta, 1921), in order to prove an age of the Ṛgveda which is not to be measured by thousands but by ten thousands, nay hundred thousands or even millions of years. He would have us believe that the Ṛgveda is "as old as the Miocene or the Pliocene epoch whose age is to be computed by some hundreds of thousands, if not, millions of years." Now, why is this impossible? First of all it is extremely doubtful whether man existed at all in the Miocene or Pliocene epoch. Most anthropologists and archæologists agree that the earliest existence of man on earth cannot be traced further than to the Quarternary or Glacial epoch. But apart from this it is absolutely impossible, that the language of the Ṛgveda should be so little different as it is from the Old Persian in the 6th century B.C. and from the Sanskrit of Pāṇini and Patanjali, if it had been the language of a people that lived even only in the quarternary, to say nothing of the Miocene or Pliocene epochs.

For languages, as a rule, change very rapidly; there are languages (and these are exceptions) that have changed comparatively little in the course of a thousand years, but never have languages been known to have remained almost unchanged for thousands or ten thousands of years. Merely from a linguistic point of view the theory of Abinas Chandra Das must be rejected. It must also be rejected from a historical point of view. Though I have insisted very often on the remoteness in age of the Ṛgvedic hymns from the rest of Indian literature yet this is only a relative remoteness. And comparatively old as the hymns of the Ṛgveda may be, yet even the earliest hymns show us Indian life, Indian thought, Indian manners and customs as not so different from those of the epics or of the classical Sanskrit literature that we could separate them from the later Indian literature even only by thousands to say nothing of ten thousands or hundred thousands of years.

To sum up the results of our investigations I should say:

1. Buddhism and Jainism presuppose the whole of the Veda. If, as it is probable, the origin of the Jaina religion goes back to Pārśva, the predecessor of Mahāvīra, the Veda must have been completed and considered as the sacred texts of Brahmanism as early as the 8th century B.C.

2. The hymns of the Ṛgveda are older than all the rest of Indian literature.

3. The origin and growth of the Ṛgveda-Saṃhitā requires a long time, several centuries.

4. The Ṛgveda-Saṃhitā is considerably older than the Atharvaveda-Saṃhitā and the Yajurveda-Saṃhitās.

5. All the Saṃhitās are older than the Brāhmaṇas.

6. Both the Brāhmaṇas and the Upanishads need a long time for their development.

7. The close relationship between the language of the Vedic Saṃhitās on the one hand and Awesta and Old Persian on the other, does not allow us to date the beginning of the Vedic period back into a hoary age of many thousands to say nothing of millions of years B.C.

8. On the other hand, the facts of political, religious and literary history require a period of at least a thousand years and probably more between the earliest hymns of the Ṛgveda and the latest parts of the old Upanishads and the rise of Buddhism.

9. It is not possible to give any definite date for the beginning of Vedic poetry. We do not know more for certain than that Vedic literature began at some unknown time in the past and extended up to the 8th century.

10. But it is more probable that this unknown time of the beginning of the Vedic literature was nearer 2500 or 2000 B.C. than to 1500 or 1200 B.C.

Personally I should prefer to mention no figures at all. We simply do not know anything more than what I said. This may be very disappointing to those of you who expected a definite answer to the question regarding the age of the oldest monument of Indian literature. But it is a greater service to Science to confess our ignorance than to deceive ourselves and others by producing dates, which are no dates. And after all, it is some comfort to know that we can set up at least some limits not only of our knowledge but also of our ignorance.

We are not allowed to let our imagination wander back into an unlimited past—from this we are prevented by historical and linguistic facts—and Buddha, Yāska and Pāṇini warn us to bring even the latest productions of Vedic literature down to a too modern time.

M. WINTERNITZ

# ASCETIC LITERATURE IN ANCIENT INDIA[1]

It has become an almost general habit, to speak of the whole of the Indian literature and culture, as far as it is pre-Buddhist, as 'Brāhmaṇical' and generally to designate as 'Brāhmaṇical' everything that is not either Buddhist or Jain just as if in ancient India all literary production and intellectual work had been confined to the priests.

Only a few scholars such as Garbe and Rhys Davids have protested against this fashion of labelling everything as 'Brāhmaṇical' and have shown, that the Kṣatriyas also had a great share in the intellectual life and work of ancient India. And years ago E. Lenmann has pointed out, that there existed in ancient India also a 'Parivrājaka literature' in which not only Brāhmaṇical but also non-Brāhmaṇical ascetics (Parivrājakas) took part and that this literature has not been entirely lost but could be gathered together from different works of literature.

Now, I believe that this Parivrājaka or Śramaṇa or ascetic literature has been preserved to us to a much greater extent, than Lenmann thought. It is to be found chiefly in the didactic parts of the Mahābhārata and occasionally also in the Purāṇas. This ascetic literature is partly pre-Buddhist and traces of it are already found in the Upaniṣads, partly contemporaneous with Buddhist and Jain literature.

If there had not been two different representatives of intellectual and spiritual life in India, how could we explain the constant occurrence of the phrase 'Samanas and Brāhmaṇas' in the Buddhist sacred texts, of Samana Bambhana in Aśoka's inscriptions, and the distinctions Megasthenes makes between 'Brāhmaṇas' and 'Sarmanas' (Brachmânai and Sarmânai).

[1] Readership lecture delivered at the Calcutta University on the 12th August, 1923.

When we examine more closely the literature of legends and poetical maxims, included in the Mahābhārata and in the Purāṇas, we shall clearly distinguish not only two different ethical systems, two different views of life, but also two distinctly different streams of literature. We shall find on the one hand Brāhmaṇical ethics, the priestly view of life, Brāhmaṇical literature, and on the other hand, ascetic morality, the ascetic view of life and ascetic literature.

And what is the difference? Brāhmaṇical legendary poetry starts from Vedic mythology. Its heroes are the Ṛṣis of old, the ancestors of the Brāhmaṇas, the founders of the great priestly families and schools. These Ṛṣis are themselves half-mythical beings who have much in common with the 'heroes' of ancient Greece. These Greek 'heroes' were a particular class of beings by the side of gods and men, men of bygone ages, famous in legend or history, who received worship as supermen as we might call them. The same is the case with the Ṛṣis in India. They too, belong to a distant past. No Ṛṣis are born in the Kali Yuga, says Āpastamba. They are a class of beings by the side of the gods whom they even assisted at the creation. In Greece it was mostly ancient kings, who became 'heroes' though Lykurg, the law-giver, and poets like Homer, Aeschylos and Sophokles also were honoured among the 'heroes,' the Indian Ṛṣis (even the Rājarṣis, the royal Ṛṣis) were above all sages, the seers of the Vedic hymns, the framers of law and ritual. As the ancestors of the Brāhmaṇical families they naturally were the heroes of Brāhmaṇical poetry.

The ethics of the legendary poetry and still more of the Brāhmaṇical gnomic poetry is entirely a priestly code of morals. It requires knowledge of the Veda, sacrifice, and honouring of the Brāhmaṇas, who are even placed above the gods. It strictly adheres to the system of castes. By 'charity' these Brāhmaṇical legends and maxims invariably mean liberality towards the Brāhmaṇas, ample gifts to the priests. Self-sacrifice means absolute devotion towards the priests. That king is praised and glorified who presents thousands of cows to the Brāhmaṇas, that king is actually raised into heaven, who is entirely obedient to the priest and humbles himself completely before the Brāhmaṇa. This ethical system also knows the ideal of renunciation of the world,—but only from the point of view of the Āśrama theory according to which the Aryan has first to pass the stage of Brahmacārin, the student of the Veda, and of the householder (gṛhastha) who founds a family, offers sacrifices, and honours the Brāhmaṇas, before he is allowed to retire from this world as an hermit or an ascetic.

Quite different is the ethical ideal of the ascetic poetry. Its legends are not based on the mythology of the Veda, but rather on the folk-lore of popular tales and ballads. The heroes of this legendary poetry are not the half-divine Ṛṣis, but the world-renouncing Yogins and ascetics. It is true, we read a great deal about Tapas, austerities, also in the Brāhmaṇical legends of the ancient Ṛṣis. But this Tapas in Brāhmaṇical literature is rather a magic power as which it is found even among primitive people but not a moral factor. Thus in Brāhmaṇical legends asceticism for the Ṛṣis is a means of obtaining supernatural powers which even makes the king of the gods tremble in his heaven. By Tapas the Ṛṣi becomes a 'Superman' who inspires fear, and may become dangerous by his curse. The cursing Ṛṣi is a typical figure in Brāhmaṇical legends. Therefore there is often something primitive about such Ṛṣis as Agastya, for instance, who swallows and digests the ocean, and is a warrior and hunter as well as an ascetic, and who has more of a Herakles than of a sage about him. On the other hand, in the ascetic poetry, asceticism is a moral factor and the hero of its legends is the saint who has renounced the world and looks upon asceticism as a means for obtaining enancipation, Mokṣa: the saint who fears no being and of whom no being is afraid.

He is a hero only in the sense of the man who goes to the utmost limit of self-denial and self-sacrifice. For this ascetic morality culminates in Ahiṁsā, abstaining from hurting any being, and in Maitrī, love of all that lives. It demands complete renunciation of this world, and it disregards caste. Not priests are the poets of these legends and maxims and the teachers of this morality, but sages of all castes and ranks.

This ascetic morality however is only part of the whole ascetic view of life which is based on the belief in transmigration and *karman*. This belief in the deed that is the fate of man and leads to the misery of Saṁsāra, to the eternal round of rebirths and redeaths (punarmṛtyu) lies at the root of that pessimism that is so characteristic of all ascetic poetry. It is full of bitter complaints about the worthlessness and transitoriness of earthly life, about old age, disease and death harassing the beings, when hurled about from existence to existence. The consciousness of this suffering to which all creatures are subject, leads to that great pity with all that lives, to the ethics of Ahiṁsā and Maitrī. But when the question is asked, what is the cause of all this suffering, the answer given—not only by the Buddhists but also by other ascetic sects—is: It is the greed, tṛṣṇā (the thirst) the unsatiable desire, that drives the beings on to every new karman and new rebirths. And lastly the other pole of the pessimistic view of life is emancipation, deliverance from saṁsāra, mokṣa and nirvāna. Hence the frequent descriptions of the bliss of tranquillity of the saint and sage whether he is called Yogin or Arhat or Kevalin or Buddha or Jaina—who has reached what is called 'Nirvāna' or 'Brahman,' or 'abode of Viṣṇu,' but is essentially one and the same thing in all ascetic literature.

These are the ideas which pervade the whole of ascetic poetry in the Mahābhārata as well as in Buddhist and Jain texts, and are found again in the Śānti and Vairāgya Śatakas of Bhartṛhari and other poets.

But all these ideas are hardly ever met with in the Veda. They are absent from the hymns and scarce in the Upaniṣads. It is true, we find, the karman doctrine in two of the oldest Upaniṣads, the Chāndogya and the Bṛhadāraṇyaka where characteristically enough it is taught by a king to the Brāhmaṇa. But it is only one of the latest Upaniṣads the Maitrāyanīya which by its style and language proves to be nearer the classical than the Vedic literature, in which we meet with all those pessimistic ideas which are so characteristic of ascetic poetry.

The two ethical ideas—the āśrama ideal of the Brāhmaṇism and the ascetic ideal are well-contrasted in one of the finest pieces of ascetic poetry—the pitāputrasaṁvāda 'dialogue between father and son' which is found twice in the Sabhāparvan of the Mahābhārata, in an expanded version in the Mārkaṇḍeya Purāṇa, and other versions of which are found in the Buddhist Jātaka and in the Uttarādhyayana Sūtra of the Jainas. (This occurrence in so many different texts proves that it is neither Buddhist nor Jain but belongs to general ascetic literature). In this dialogue the son denounces this world which is harassed by death and decay, and praises the ascetic life, while the father admonishes him to stick to the Brāhmaṇical ideal, according to which Veda study, family life, and religious rites should be practised in youth and ascetic life and renunciation of this life only in old age. Let me quote part of this dialogue from Muir's translation from the Mahābhārata:

*Son.*

Since soon the days of mortals end,  
How ought the wise their lives to spend?  
What course should I, to duty true,  
My sire, from youth to age pursue?

*Father.*

Begin thy course with study; store  
The mind with holy Vedic lore.

That stage completed, seek a wife,
And gain the fruit of wedded life,
A race of sons, by rites to seal,
When thou art gone, thy spirit's weal.
Then light the sacred fires, and bring
The gods a fitting offering.
When age draws nigh, the world forsake
Thy chosen home the forest make;
And there a calm, ascetic sage,
A war against thy passions wage,
That, cleansed from every earthly stain,
Thou may'st supreme perfection gain.

*Son.*

And art thou then, my father, wise,
When thou dost such a life advise?
What wise or thoughtful man delights
In formal studies, empty rites?
Should such pursuits and thoughts engage
A mortal more than half his age?
The world is ever vexed, distressed;
The noiseless robbers never rest.

*Father.*

Tell how the world is vexed, distressed;
What noiseless robbers never rest?
What means thy dark, alarming speech?
In plainer words thy meaning teach.

*Son.*

The world is vexed by death; decay
The frames of mortals wear away.
Dost thou not note the circling flight
Of those still robbers, day and night,
With stealthy tread which hurrying past
Steal all our lives away at last?............

No moment lose; in serious mood
Begin at once to practise good;
To-morrow's task to-day conclude;
The evening's work complete at noon:
No duty can be done too soon.
Who knows whom death may seize to-night,
And who shall see the morning light?
And death will never stop to ask,
If thou hast done or not, thy task.
While yet a youth, from folly cease;
Through virtue seek for calm and peace.
So shalt thou here attain renown
And future bliss thy lot shall crown............
Thou dost advise, that I should please
With sacrifice the deities.
Such rites I disregard as vain;
Through these can none perfection gain.
Why sate the gods, at cruel feasts
With flesh and blood of slaughtered beasts?
Far other sacrifices I
Will offer unremittingly;
The sacrifice of calm, of truth,
The sacrifice of peace, of ruth,
Of life serenely, purely spent,
Of thought profound on Brahma bent.
Who offers these may death defy,
And hope for immortality.
And then thou say'st that I should wed
And sons should gain to tend me dead
By offering pious gifts, to seal,
When I am gone, my spirit's weal.
But I shall ask no pious zeal
Of sons to guard my future weal.
No child of mine shall ever boast
His rites have saved his father's ghost

Of mine own bliss I'll pay the price
And be myself my sacrifice."

There are indications enough that this ascetic poetry had its origin in non-Brāhmaṇical circles. It cannot be a mere accident that in the Mahābhārata the persons who teach this ascetic morality are as a rule not Brāhmaṇas. Thus it is Vidura who is very often made the mouth-piece for maxims and legends of ascetic poetry. Though this Vidura lived at the court of Dhṛtarāṣṭra and was highly respected, his low origin is frequently alluded to. He converses with Yudhiṣṭhira in language unintelligible to others contrary to the rule found in the Mahābhārata and already in the Śatapatha-Brāhmaṇa, that Aryans should not speak barbarian languages (nāryā mlecchantibhāṣāh). Being himself the son of a slave girl, he also marries a Pārasava maiden, that is, the offspring of a king begotten on a Śūdra woman. In the Jātaka where he is called Vidura or Vidhura and always appears as the prototype of wisdom, he once quotes two verses in which four kinds of slaves are enumerated, and adds: "I am myself 'slave by birth' (addha hi yonito aham pi jāto), just as in the Mahābhārata (5, 40, 5) he says शूद्रयोनावहं जात :

Long didactic sections are put in the mouth of Vidura, so the Vidurahitavākya (5, 32-40). Though the majority of the verses in the section contain general rules of morality and wisdom, it also contains a great number of verses which teach what I call ascetic morality—verses which sound quite Buddhistic and some of which have actually been traced in the Pāli canon.

Another great section in which Vidura is the speaker, is the Dhṛtarāṣṭraśokapanodana in the Strīparvan (2-7) where Vidura tries to comfort Dhṛtarāṣṭra about the loss of his sons. He describes here the misery of Saṁsāra and the power of death and fate. Here he relates the famous parable of 'the Man in the Well.'

A Brāhmaṇa once lost his way in a dense forest full of beasts of prey. In great terror he ran about, looking in vain for a way out. Then he saw that the terrible forest was surrounded on all sides by traps, and, that a dreadful-looking woman encircled it with both her arms. Five-headed dragons, big and horrible to look at, and rising like rocks to the sky, surrounded this great forest. And in the middle of this forest there was a well, covered over with underwood and creepers. The Brāhmaṇa fell intoit, and remained hanging in the branches of a creeper. As the large fruit of a bread-fruit tree, held by its stalk, hangs down, so he was hanging there, feet upwards, head downwards. And yet another, even greater, danger threatens him there. In the middle of the well he perceives a big and mighty serpent, and from one end of the covering of the well he sees a giant elephant, black, with six mouths and twelve feet, slowly approaching. But in the branches of the tree that covered the well, all kinds of horrible bees were swarming and prepared honey. And as the honey was dripping down, it was greedily swallowed by the man hanging in the well. For he was not weary of existence and did not give up the hope of life, even though white and black mice also were gnawing the tree on which he hang.

The parable is thus explained by Vidura: The forest is the Saṁsāra, the round of existences in this world; the beasts of prey are the diseases; the hideous giant woman is old age; the well is the body; the dragon at the bottom of the well is Time; the creepers in which the man is hanging is the hope of life; the elephant with six mouths and twelve feet is the Year with its six seasons and twelve months, the black and white mice are the nights and the days, and the honey drops are the sensual pleasures.

There can be no doubt that this parable is a genuine production of Ancient Indian ascetic poetry. It has sometimes been called a Buddhist parable, but it is no more in accordance with the Buddhist view of life than that of the Jains or any other ascetic sect of India. A Jain version of the parable is found in the Dharmaparīkṣā of the Digambara Amitagati (1017 A. D.) and again in the Sthavirāvalicarita of the famous Jain monk Hemacandra (12th cent.). Buddhist versions are found in Avadānas known from Chinese translations. And it must be through some Buddhist version that it found its way into the Buddhist Christian legend book 'Barlaam and Joasaph' and the world-known fable book 'Kalilag and Damnag.' The Persian Sufi poet Jelal-ed-din Rumi translated it into Persian, from which P. Ruckert rendered it into German in a poem which is well-known to every child in Germany. It has wandered to many peoples and has equally served for the edification of the Brāhmaṇas, Buddhists, and Jains, as of Mahomedans, Jews and Christians.

But that it is neither Buddhist nor Jain in origin, but belongs to an earlier stratum of ascetic poetry is shown by its appearance in Vidura's discourse of consolation. For after relating this parable, Vidura continues to teach love, kindness and pity towards all beings as the only way that leads out of the Saṁsāra, which is here called the way to Brahman or to the eternal abode of Viṣṇu, though it is described in the same way as the Buddhist Nirvāna.

In other cases also we find men of despised caste or of low rank as teachers of ascetic morality. Thus in the Vanaparvan (207-216) the Brāhmaṇa Kauśika is instructed by the pious hunter and dealer in meat Dharmavyādha on philosophy and ethics, and is taught that a man is a true Brāhmaṇa not by birth but by virtuous conduct. The pious woman who has sent him to the Dharmavyādha also recites (III. 206-8) a number of verses with the refrain तं देवा ब्राह्मणं विदुः 'Him the gods know to be a Brāhmaṇa,' namely, him who gives up wrath and ignorance—him who having himself been injured, never injures others, who has his passions all controlled, etc. Similar passages (with the refrain : tam aham brūmi brahmanam, 'him I call a Brāhmaṇa' occur also in the

Udāna of the Buddhists. And also in the Śāntiparvan (251-10) it is said—exactly as in Buddhist maxim—that one does not become a Brāhmaṇa by Veda study and sacrifice, but only by giving up all desires and by kindness towards all beings.

Another important piece of ascetic poetry in the Mahābhārata is the Tulādhāra-Jājali Saṁvāda, the narrative dialogue between Jājali and Tulādhāra (Śāntipārvan, 261-264), in which again a man of low caste, the pedlar Tulādhāra, teaches the Brāhmaṇa Jājali the eternal law of love (maitrī) and non-violence (ahiṁsā).

Very often the teachings of ascetic morality are mixed up with those of Brāhmaṇical ethics and it is not always easy to decide, whether we have to see in such passages an attempt at a compromise between the two different views of life or rather the retouching of an old piece of ascetic poetry at the hands of some Brāhmaṇical editor. Thus in the Dharmavyādha section from which I have just quoted, the pious hunter preaches Ahiṁsā but tries to bring it into harmony with the requirements of the Brāhmaṇical cult.

Certainly the Ahiṁsā doctrine, the most essential part of ascetic morality, is absolutely incompatible with the animal sacrifice of Brāhmaṇic rites. There are several passages in the Mokṣadharma of the Mahābhārata where the slaying of animals for sacrifice is absolutely denounced, while in other passages both Ahiṁsā and the observances of Vedic rites are taught at the same time.

A pure piece of ascetic poetry are the verses sung by king Vicakhnu (Mahābhārat, XII, 265) 'out of compassion for the creatures' (प्रजानामनुकम्पार्थम्). When he sees a bull being prepared for sacrifice, he denounces the slaying of animals and teaches that Ahiṁsā is the highest law, which Manu himself is said to have declared to be the very soul of religion. सर्वकर्मस्वहिंसाहि धर्मात्मा मनुरब्रवीत्. Mark that it is a king and not a Brāhmaṇa who teaches this lesson.

[1] Hebrew versions in the fables of Rabbi Barachia Nikdani (1661).

Again in the Yajñanindā chapter (Mbh. XII. 272): A Brāhmaṇa who according to his vow offers only vegetable sacrifices, is tempted by an antelope, by the goddess Sāvitrī, and by the sight of the heavenly world with its Apsaras, to make his sacrifice complete by animal offering. But the moment he desires to slay the antelope, the fruit of his asceticism (तपस्) vanishes from him and the antelope who is in reality God Dharma in disguise, teaches him that slaying cannot be part of worship (तस्मात् हिंसा न यज्ञिया) for: 'Non-violence is the whole religion' (Ahiṁsā sakalo dharmaḥ).

Very interesting is the Gokapilīya section in the same book of the Mahābhārata (XII. 269-71). The Yati Kapila sees a cow that is to be slain for sacrifice, and exclaims: 'Alas, the Vedas' (वेदाः इति). On hearing this, the Risi Syūmaraśmi enters into the body of the cow, and asks Kapila, what better doctrines he would substitute for the Veda. Kapila begins his answer with the words: 'I do not blame the Vedas,' yet the tenor of his answer is directed against the Veda. And in the whole lengthy dialogue Syūmaraśmi consistently defends the Vedic point of view, while Kapila is entirely inconsistent in teaching Ahiṁsā, resignation and knowledge as the only road to Mokṣa, and at the same time acknowledging Vedic rites and ceremonies. We know from many examples in Indian literature from the Upaniṣads and the Buddhist Suttas down to the works of Śaṅkara, that the art of dialectics was highly developed in India, that Indian Philosophers always were good debaters. And if we find such a poor piece of dialectics as the Gokapilīya is, it seems to me perfectly clear, that we have a piece of ancient ascetic poetry that has been entirely spoiled by the Brāhmaṇical editor.

Another example for such attempts at Brāhmaṇising original ascetic poetry is the interesting dialogue between an adhvaryu, a sacrificial priest and a Yati, an ascetic, in the Anugītā (Mbh. XIV. 28, 6 ff.). Here the ascetic reproaches the priest that he was committing the sin of violence (hiṁsā) by immolating a he-goat. To this the priest replies: The he-goat is not destroyed by being sacrificed, on the contrary he attains highest bliss, for it is said in the Veda: 'That part of it which is of the substance of earth goes to the earth; that which is of the substance of water goes to the waters; its eye goes to the sun, its ear to the quarters, and its breath to heaven.' Whereupon the ascetic replies; "If you think that this he-goat by being deprived of life attains highest bliss, then the sacrifice is offered for the sake of the he-goat, what use it is then to you? And besides, however that may be, you would have to consult with the brother, the father, the mother and all the kindred to the he-goat, whether they agree to his being slain.' The Adhvaryu has practically nothing to reply to this. But the curious thing is, that the author of the Anugītā represents the Adhvaryu as the victor in the debate, while the unbiassed reader certainly has the impression that the ascetic is right. This is, no doubt, due to the Brāhmaṇical editor having retouched the dialogue which originally was nothing but a piece of ascetic poetry.

For in many other passages also the Anugītā enjoins the law of Ahiṁsā. It says, f.i. (14, 50, 2 ff.) that Ahiṁsā is the highest law, knowledge the highest good and those who defend the slaying of animals at sacrifice will go to hell as Nāstikas. And there are many passages which are in full agreement with the Buddhist and Jain ideas. What the Siddha says at the very beginning of the Anugītā could have been said by Mahāvīra in any Jain text, or by the Tathāgata in any Buddhist Sutta. Even terms like tṛṣṇā, saṁskāra, nirvāna are used quite in the Buddhist sense. The 'Gāthās sung by king Ambarīṣa' (quoted 14, 31, 5 ff.) in which avidity (lobha) and greed (tṛṣṇā) are said to be the worst enemies of man that must be eradicated with the sword, sound Buddhist. And king Janaka also speaks like a Buddhist when he says (14, 32) that he cannot call anything his own, that nothing belongs to him and quotes, as from the Veda, though it is not to be found in it, a saying 'whose is this, whose is my own?' (कस्येदमिति कस्य स्वमिति). And as in the Buddhist Suttas it is so often said that he is wise and emancipated for whom there is no 'Ego' and no 'mine' so we read in the Anugītā (14, 51, 29): 'Two syllables mean death, three syllables 'the eternal Brahman.' '(मम)' 'mine' means 'death' '(न मम)' 'not mine' 'the eternal.'

But also in the Śāntiparvan and other didactic parts of the Mahābhārata we find numerous verses which remind us of similar verses in the Pāli Tipiṭaka, and quite a number of verses of the Mahābhārata have actually been found almost verbally in Buddhist texts.

Thus we read in the Śāntiparvan the famous saying of Janaka of Videha (अनन्तं बत मे वित्तं यस्य मे नास्ति किंचन। मिथिलायां प्रदीप्तायां न मे दह्यति किंचन।

"Infinite wealth is mine, as I possess nothing, if Mithilā burns down, nothing is burnt that is mine" (Mahābhārat XII. 178). The same verse is found in the Jātaka and in a Jain legend. Again we are reminded of the Taṇhāvagga in the Dhammapada, when we read verses as the following in the Mahābhārata.[1]

"All the happiness consisting in the fulfilment of one's desires, and whatever bliss there may be in heaven, all that is not worth the sixteenth part of the bliss consisting in the annihilation of greed (tṛṣṇā)."

"That disease, of which the fool never gets rid, that does not grow old with old age, that disease which only ends with life itself—it is greed (tṛṣṇā), happy the man who frees himself from it."

"As the tailor with his needle passes the thread through the garment, so the thread web of Saṁsāra is passed through the needle of greed (tṛṣṇā)."

[1] XII, 174, 46, 55, 21F, 36.

"As the horn of a cow grows at the same rate as the cow grows, so greed (tṛṣnā) grows at the same rate as wealth grows."

There is a famous legend found both in the Mahābhārata and in the Purāṇas, the legend of Yayāti, which has been made the vehicle for conveying the same lesson of ascetic morality that is expressed in these verses. Yayāti is not a Brāhmaṇical hero. He belongs to a race of kings who were hostile to the Brāhmaṇas: His grand-father Purūravas oppressed the Brāhmaṇas and was therefore cursed by the Ṛṣis.[1] His father Nahuṣa went so far as to tax the Ṛṣis and even to ride on their backs. Even in heaven, after having conquered Indra, he yoked the heavenly Ṛṣis before his chariot, and set his foot on the head of Agastya, who cursed him that he fell down from heaven and had to live on earth as a snake for 10,000 years. Yayāti, the son of Nahuṣa, had two wives, one was the daughter of the Asura King, the other that of the Asura priest Sukra. Even towards this Asura priest he behaved badly, and was cursed by him that he should lose his youth and become old at once. But he was allowed to confer his old age on somebody else. His youngest son Pūru is prepared to bestow his youth on his father and take old age from him. Thus Yayāti having become young again enjoys life and all sensual pleasures once more for a thousand years to the full but he never is satiated. And at last after a thousand years he becomes aware of the truth which he expresses in the verses:

"Verily, not by satisfying desires, is craving ever appeased: No, it only grows and becomes stronger, as fire by ghee poured into it. Even the whole earth, filled with treasures, gold and cattle and women, they are not enough for one man:—Considering this, seek calmness of mind. Only he, who never injures any being by deeds or thoughts or words,—becomes one with the Brahman. He who fears nothing, and

[1] Mahābhārata 4, F5.

of whom no being is ever afraid, he who desires nothing, and knows no hatred,—becomes one with the Brahman." With these thoughts he returns his youth to his son Pūru, taking his own old age from him and having placed Pūru on the throne he goes to the forest and devotes himself to rigorous austerities for a thousand years.

Windisch[1] has once referred to this legend as 'having a Buddhist character,' and has pointed out a parallel to the pada: पृकस्यापिनपयासिं in the Mārasamyukta of the Divyāvadāna. I see in it an old folk tale reminding us of the Greek Titan myths, that was converted into a piece of ascetic poetry.

The Mahābhārata, and more specially the Mokṣadharma of the Śāntiparvan, is full of legends and moral maxims which have all the appearance of being Jain or Buddhist in their origin, but which at any rate cannot be called Brāhmaṇical. Take for instance, the story of the huntsman and the doves (Śānti-parvan 143-149).[2] This 'sacred sin-destroying Itihāsa' relates how the wicked hunter has caught a female dove and how the husband of this dove burns himself in the fire for the wicked hunter who has caught his beloved wife only because he has no other food to offer to him whom he considered as his 'guest,' how the dove follows her husband into death, whereupon the wicked hunter deeply touched, gives up his wild life, becomes an ascetic and finally also seeks death in the fire. This story might be of Jain origin, as the Jainas approve of religious suicide. At any rate it is not 'Brāhmaṇical.'

Another side of the ascetic view of life is illustrated in the story of Mudgala (Mahābhārata 3, 260 f.). The ascetic Mudgala is very wise and pious, and one day a messenger of the gods appears, to lead him up to heaven. But Mudgala is cautious enough to enquire of the messenger, what kind of

[1] Māra and Buddha, p. 108A.

[2] It is also found in the Jaina recension of the Pañcatantra.

life it is that awaits the beings in heaven. The messenger describes all the glories of heaven and the bliss that awaits the pious there. He cannot, however, conceal from him the fact that this bliss is not of eternal duration. Everyone must reap the fruit of his actions. When once the Karman is exhausted, one has to descend again from heaven and begin a new life. Thereupon Mudgala does not want to hear any more of heaven. He devotes himself again to ascetic practices, and finally through deep meditation (dhyānayoga) and complete indifference towards the world of senses attains to the highest place of Viṣṇu in which alone the bliss of Nirvāna is to be found.

Another hero of ascetic poetry, who not only refuses heaven, but even prefers hell to it, is king Vipaścit ('the wise one') in the beautiful legend told in the Mārkaṇḍeya-Purāṇa:

Vipaścit has been pious and virtuous all his life, yet after his death, he is led by Yama's attendant into hell. The king is much surprised at that, but the attendant tells him that once he has committed a slight transgression of one of the rules prescribed by Brāhmaṇic religion and according to the law of Karman he must stay in hell for a very short time. And after a few minutes he turns to lead the king out of hell to his well-deserved abode in heaven. The king is about to go, when he hears horrible wailing and the dwellers in hell beseech and implore him to stay one moment longer, for a wondrously pleasant breath emanated from him appeasing the tortures of hell. Yama's attendant explains to the king, that from the noble deeds of a good man a refreshing breath emanates that is soothing to the tortured in hell. On hearing this the king staunchly refuses to go to heaven. For, he says in a magnificent dialogue, not in heaven nor in Brahman's world is there such bliss for men as in helping those who are suffering. In vain he is first told by Yama's attendant, then by Yama himself and even by god

Indra, that every man must receive the reward or the punishment of his good or evil deeds. The king insists on his remaining in hell, as long as he can assuage the suffering of the poor dwellers in hell, who for him are not sinners but sufferers. He only leaves hell, when the lord of the gods promises him, that by his good works the denizens of hell will be released from their pain.

King Vipaścit is a counterpart, perhaps a forerunner of the Bodhisattva Avalokiteśvara in Mahāyāna Buddhism, but he is certainly not a Brāhmaṇical hero.

In Brahmanical legends, too, we hear of kings who perform wonderful feats of self-denial, self-sacrifice and self-humiliation. You will know the stories of king Śibi who in Buddhist legends pulls out his eyes to give them to a blind beggar or gives up his body for the welfare of men and beasts. In the Mahābhārata too an Itihāsa is told of this king who gives up his flesh and blood, to save the life of a pigeon, and to satisfy the hawk whom he has deprived of his food (Mbh. III. 100 f., 197; XIII. 32). This is genuine ascetic poetry. But in another passage of the Mahābhārata [1] we are told that this same king Śibi as a pious sacrificer presented to the priests so many cows as rain-drops fall to the ground, as there are stars in the sky, and grains of sand in the bed of the Ganges. And again in another passage [2] this king Śibi is represented as a model king, because he slaughters his own son Bṛhadgarbha and cooks his flesh and is even prepared to eat the flesh of his son—only because he is ordered to do so by a Brāhmaṇa and for this glorious deed of devotion to the priests he went from this world straight to heaven (नाकपृष्ठ मितोगतः). Here you see the great difference between ascetic and Brāhmaṇic legendary poetry most clearly.

I am afraid, I have taxed your patience already too long. But what I said, will suffice to show that there was in ancient

[1] III. 58.

[2] III. 198; *cf.* XII. 234, 19.

India an ascetic literature different in its character and in its teaching entirely from the Brāhmaṇic literature.

The question arises : What is the historical position of this ancient Indian ascetic poetry ?

As a matter of fact, this ascetic poetry is found chiefly in the didactic portions of the Mahābhārata in connection with the psychological and metaphysical doctrines of Sāṁkhya and Yoga, besides largely in Buddhist and Jain Literature. And it will be found that the ideas and ideals of this ascetic poetry are organically connected with Sāṁkhya and Yoga as well as with Buddhism and Jainism while whenever they appear mixed up with orthodox Brāhmaṇism in Brāhmaṇical literature they appear as something foreign.

Now if it were proved or could be proved that the didactic sections of the Mahābhārata especially the Mokṣadharma and the Anugītā, are pre-Buddhist and belong to the 6th century B. C., then we could say that ascetic legends and moral tales and maxims found in the Mahābhārata are the source from which the ascetic poetry of the Buddhists and Jains is derived. But a careful study of the Mahābhārata has shown that the didactic sections belong to the the latest, not the oldest, stratum of the Mahābhārata, and that the teaching contained in them is not a uniform system of philosophy as it is sometimes called,—but rather a jumble of the most different philosophical teaching of different times. It is, therefore, impossible to fix the ascetic poetry of the Mahābhārata chronologically. All we can say, is that many of the Itihāsas and moral maxims of the Mahābhārata may have existed and probably did exist independently or as parts of other works long before they came to be included in the great epic, while others are of later growth.

I am inclined to think that ascetic poetry and the peculiar view of life expressed in it, first arose in an old form of Yoga which was merely a system of ethics and a practical theory of redemption, that could as easily be combined with Sāṁkhya, as with Buddhist and Jain teaching. Both Sāṁkhya and Yoga though taken up into the folds of orthodox Brāhmaṇism were originally not Brāhmaṇical, but independent of the Veda.

At any rate, it is worth mentioning that wherever Sāṁkhya doctrines are taught in the Mahābhārata, as in the Mokṣadharma and in the Anugītā, it is only the ethical teaching, the Yoga element, to which we find so many parallels in Buddhist literature. Take for instance, the teaching of Pañcaśikha (Pañcaśikhavākya) in the Mokṣadharma (Mahābhārata XII. 218-220). Pañcaśikha is the teacher of Janaka of Videha, and the pupil of Āsuri, the pupil of Kapila. All that he teaches about ethics is hardly different from the teaching of Buddha and most of the maxims found in the Pañcaśikhavākya are such as we are wont to find in the Dhammapada or Suttanipāta or any other Buddhist text. On the other hand, of all that he says about the Guṇas, Buddhi, Manas and other peculiar Sāṁkhya doctrines, nothing is to be found in Buddhism or Buddhist literature.

But some of the legends and maxims of the ascetic poetry contained in the epic are doubtless borrowed from Jain or Buddhist texts. As it is, whenever we find the same legend or maxim both in the Mahābhārata and in Buddhist and Jain texts there are two possibilities :

(1) The original may have been either Buddhist or Jain ; or (2) The parallel passages may all go back to the same source, an older ascetic literature, that probably arose in connection with Yoga or Sāṁkhya-Yoga teaching.

It will have to be decided in each individual case, whether the one or the other is more probable. A wide field of research opens here to students of the Mahābhārata, and of Jain and Buddhist literature. This research is not only necessary for the history of Indian literature, but will also throw considerable light on the history of Indian ethics.

M. Winternitz

# ANCIENT INDIAN BALLAD POETRY

I said in my first lecture that the Ṛgveda-Saṃhitā contains, besides the sacrificial hymns which form the nucleus of the collection, also some remnants of ancient poetry that was unconnected with religious rites. Among these are about twenty poems, which are legends, myths or stories in the form of dialogues and may be called *Saṃvāda* or *Ākhyāna*, or *Itihāsa hymns*.

These are poems consisting entirely of dialogues or conversations. The best known specimen of this kind of poetry is the Saṃvāda between *Purūravas and Urvaśī* (Rv. X, 95): Purūravas is a mortal, Urvaśī an Apsaras or nymph.

During four years the beautiful Apsaras lived on earth as the wife of Purūravas, until she became with child. Then she vanished 'like the first of the dawns.' Thereupon he went forth to seek her. At last he finds her, as she is playing on a lake with other water nymphs. This is about all that we can gather from the dark and often unintelligible verses, containing the conversation between the deserted Purūravas and the goddess who is amusing herself with her playmates in the pond. Fortunately this ancient myth of the love of a mortal king for a divine maiden is also preserved to us in other works of Indian literature, so that we are able, at least to a certain extent, to reconstruct the story underlying the conversation between Purūravas and Urvaśī. In the Śatapatha Brāhmaṇa (XI, 6, 1) the story is told that Urvaśī, when she consented to become the wife of Purūravas, stipulated three conditions, one of them being that she must never see him naked. The Gandharvas, however, denizens of the same heavenly world to which the Apsarases belong, want Urvaśī to come back to heaven. Therefore, one night they rob the two little lambs which Urvaśī loves like children and which are tied to her bed. And as Urvaśī complains bitterly that she was being robbed as if there were no man there, Purūravas jumped up 'naked as he was,' for it seemed to him too long to put on a garment first, 'to pursue the thieves.' But at the same instant the Gandharvas caused a flash of lightning to appear so that of a sudden it was as bright as daylight, and Urvaśī perceived the king naked. Then she vanished, and when Purūravas came again, she was gone. Mad with grief, the king then wandered about the country, until one day he came to a pond in which nymphs in the shape of swans were swimming about. And now the conversation sets in that has been preserved in the Ṛgveda, and is repeated in the Brāhmaṇa with some explanatory remarks added. But in vain are all the pleadings of Purūravas, that she might return to him again. Even when in despair he talks of self-destruction—he would throw himself from the rocks as a prey to the fierce wolves; she has only the answer:

> "Die not Purūravas, do not throw yourself
> Down from the rock, a prey to the fierce wolves.
> There is, forsooth, no friendship with womenfolk
> For they have hearts like wild hyenas."

Whether and how Purūravas was united with his beloved is not quite clear either from the Ṛgveda Saṃvāda or from the Śatapatha Brāhmaṇa. It seems that he was transformed into a Gandharva and attained heaven, where the happiness of reunion awaited him.

The story of Purūravas and Urvaśī has been retold in India over and over again. It is alluded to in the Kāṭhaka of the Black Yayurveda, it is found in the Harivaṃśa, in the Viṣṇu Purāṇa and in the Kathāsaritsāgara and it forms the subject of one of Kālidāsa's immortal dramas. Ever so many attempts have been made by scholars to explain the verses of the Ṛgveda with the help of the later stories, but we are still far from understanding the Saṃvāda fully. This shows again, how far remote in time the Ṛgveda is from all the later literature. But another cause of not understanding the poem fully is its fragmentary character. And this is the case with the Saṃvāda hymns.

Take one other famous dialogue of the Ṛgveda, that between *Yama and Yāmī* (Rv. X, 10). The story underlying this conversation is an old myth of the origin of the human race from a first pair of twins. Yāmī tries to tempt her brother Yama to incest, in order that the human race may not die out. In passionate words glowing with love the sister invites her brother's embrace. In gentle, deliberate speech, pointing to the eternal laws of the gods which forbid the union of blood-relations, Yama repulses her :

> " Not such a friendship does thy friend desire,
> Where she of kindred blood becomes a stranger
> The watchers of the heavens see afar and wide.
> The mighty sons of the Great God."

Yāmī, however, tries to persuade her brother that the gods themselves desire that he should unite himself with her, in order to propagate his race. But as he will not listen she grows more and more persistent, more and more passionate. Finally she bursts out in wild words of abuse reviling him as being a weakling and accuses him of wishing to embrace another woman, 'like the girth embraces the horse, the creeper the tree.' Whereupon Yama concludes the dialogue with the words:

> " Thou too, O Yāmī, embrace another,
> And that other thee as the creeper clasps the tree.
> Win thou his heart, let him win thine,
> And live with him in happiest harmony."

The dialogue is full of dramatic vigour. But in this poem, too, much is still unintelligible, and it is only a fragment of a story, though a fragment of a work which certainly was one of the first pieces of poetry in the whole of Indian literature.

Now, these Saṃvāda (or Ākhyāna) hymns have been the subjects of much discussion among scholars; they form one of the great problems of Indian literature, and are of the greatest importance for the history of Indian literature, because they throw considerable light on the origin of both epic and of the dramatic poetry.

About forty years ago H. Oldenberg first started a theory about these Saṃvāda hymns, in order to explain their fragmentary and enigmatic character. He said: The oldest form of epic poetry in India was the Ākhyāna, a tale in a mixture of prose and verse, the speeches of the persons only being in verses, while the events connected with the speeches were narrated in prose. But originally only the verses used to be committed to memory and handed down, while the prose story was left to be narrated by every reciter in his own words. Now in the Ākhyāna hymns of the Ṛgveda (as he called them), only the verse portions containing the speeches of the persons have been preserved, while the prose portions of the narrative, as they were not handed down in any fixed form, are lost to us. Only some of these narratives we can partly restore with the help of the Brāhmaṇas or the epic literature, or even of commentaries. Where these helps fail, nothing remains for us but to try to guess the story from the speeches. This theory was supported by the fact that not only in Indian but also in other literatures, the mixture of prose and verse is an early form of epic poetry. We find this form, for instance, in Old Irish and in Skandinavian poetry. In India we find it in some narrative portions of the Brāhmaṇas and Upaniṣads. The story of Purūravas and Urvaśī is told in the Śatapatha Brāhmaṇa in prose with the verses of the Ṛgveda, the Uktapratyukta, as part of the Ākhyana. In the Śunaḥśepa Ākhyāna of the Aitareya-Brāhmaṇa we have also a prose story with verses (gāthā and ṛc) forming part of the Ākhyāna. In some old parts of the Mahābhārata, in the Buddhist Tripiṭaka, in the narrative literature of fables and tales, in the drama, and again in the Campu the mixture of prose and verse is an acknowledged and well established literary form. It is true that in all these cases the prose has been handed down together with the verses. But as the Ṛgveda professedly is the Veda of the Ṛc, that is of the verses, it was not possible to include any prose in the Saṃhitā of the Ṛgveda. And if an Ākhyāna consisting of prose and verse was to find a place in the Ṛgveda Saṃhitā, the prose portion would have to be omitted. Thus the theory propounded by Oldenberg seemed very plausible and for a long time it was almost generally accepted by scholars.

But of late the theory has also met with a great deal of opposition. Many years back Max Müller and Sylvain Lèvi had already suggested that the dialogue poems of the Ṛgveda might be a kind of drama. This idea has been taken up by Joh. Hertel and L. Von Schroeder who tried to prove that these Saṃvāda hymns are really dialogues belonging to some *dramatic* performances connected with the religious cult. We have only, they say, to supply dramatic action, and the difficulties which these hymns offer to interpretation will disappear. What kind of action has to be supplied can of course only be guessed from the dialogues themselves.

I believe that there is some truth in both theories. First of all, it must be remembered as we shall see that poems like the dialogue hymns of the Ṛgveda occur very frequently in Indian literature. We find similar *half-epic half-dramatic* poems, consisting chiefly or entirely of dialogues or conversations in the Mahābhārata, in the Purāṇas and specially in Buddhist literature. Some scholars are inclined to see in all these poems a more or less developed dramatic poetry. But surely a poem consisting of dialogues or speeches may appear very dramatic, but it cannot be called a real drama produced on a stage by actors. The dialogue-form is indeed, the most popular form of early narrative poetry. We find half narrative, half philosophical dialogues in the Upaniṣads, in the Mahābhārata and in the Tripiṭaka. In fact, the whole of the Mahābhārata and all the Purāṇas are dialogues or dialogues in dialogues. We often read in the didactic parts of the Mahābhārata the phrase: "Here they tell the following tale (itihāsa)," but what follows is a dialogue, a Saṃvāda. Therefore the stories of the Mahābhārata are often called "Itihāsa-Saṃvāda." And not only in India the dialogue is the favourite form of narrative and didactic poetry, it is so in the oldest literatures of other nations also. I mention only the Gilgamesh epic of the Babylonians, the Ægyptian Book of the Dead, the Zend-Avesta with its conversations between Zarathushtra and Ahura Mazda, the Book of Job in the Hebrew Bible. In Teutonic poetry we find that *the older* an epical poem is, the more space is taken up by conversations.

The Saṃvāda hymns of the Ṛgveda are then, in my opinion, nothing else but *ancient ballads* of the same kind as are found also in the literatures of many other peoples. This ancient *ballad poetry* is at once the source both of the epic and of the dramatic poetry. For these ballads consist of a narrative and of a dramatic element. The epic arose from the narrative, the drama from the dramatic elements of the ancient ballad. And these ancient Ākhyānas or ballads were not always composed entirely in verse but sometimes an introductory or a concluding story was told in prose, and occasionally the verses were linked together by short explanations in prose. So far the old theory of Oldenberg may have some justification. But most of these hymns were simply *ballads* of the *half-epic, half-dramatic* type, though not real dramas, as some scholars have thought them to be.

Such ballads which treated of one and the same subject were often combined into a cycle. And such cycles of ballads formed the nucleus, from which the epic has developed.

Thus there existed once a cycle of ballads on the great war between Pāṇḍavas and Kauravas, out of which some great poet shaped the great epic Mahābhārata in its original form, when it was a heroic poem only, and not yet an encyclopædia of religion, law and ancient lore, as it is now.

And so also the Rāmāyaṇa was based on ancient ballads on Rāma and Rāvaṇa. Happily one such ballad has been preserved to us in the Gāthās of the Daśaratha Jātaka, which contain the discourse by which Rāma comforts his brother Bharata on the death of their father Daśaratha. Though these Gāthās or verses are included in the Buddhist Jātaka book, they have nothing to do with Buddhism, but belong to non-Buddhist ballad poetry, to a cycle of ballads on the Rāma story. The ballad found its way into the Tripiṭaka on account of the ideas on the transitoriness of life and the inevitableness of death,—always a favourite theme with the Buddhists.

It is in Buddhist literature that this ballad poetry is met with most frequently. Long before there existed a connected story of the life of the Buddha, scenes from the life of the Master formed the subject of sacred ballads. They are found both in the Pali Tripiṭaka and in texts of other sects, the Mahāvastu and Lalitavistara, which proves that they belong to the earliest Buddha poetry. Three of these sacred ballads are found in the Suttanipāta: the Nālakasutta, the Pabbajjāsutta, and the Padhānasutta. The first of these ballads refers to the time immediately after the birth of the child that is to be the future Buddha:

The gods in heaven are in a state of pleasant excitement. The divine Ṛsi Asita becomes aware of their outbursts of joy, and in answer to his question, receives the reply that in the Lumbini grove in the town of the Śākyas the Buddha has just been born for the salvation of the world. Then the sage descends from heaven to the palace of Śuddhodana and requests to see the newly born boy.

"Then the Śākyas showed to Asita the child, the prince who was like shining gold, manufactured by a very skilful smith in the mouth of a forge, and beaming in glory and having a beautiful appearance.

"Seeing the prince shining like fire, bright like the bull of the stars wandering in the sky, like the burning sun in autumn, free from clouds, he joyfully obtained great delight."

And while invisible divine beings fan the child with sunshades and yaktails, the Ṛṣi Asita takes the child in his arms and calls out: "Without superior is this, the most excellent of men." But at the same moment he thinks of his own imminent end and bursts into tears. In consternation the Śākyas ask whether any evil threatens the boy. The sage reassures them. The boy will reach the summit of complete enlightenment. But he himself will not live to hear the preaching of the Buddha; therefore he is sorrowful. Before he departs, he exhorts his nephew Nālaka to follow the Buddha, as soon as his call will be heard.[1]

The second of these poems, the Pabbajjāsutta, describes the pabbajjā, that is the pravrajyā or departure from his home, of the youth Gotama and the meeting which, wandering as a mendicant ascetic, he had with the king of Rājagaha.

The third ballad, the *Padhānasutta* describes the episode how Māra, the Evil One, after having seven years followed Gotama step by step and tried in vain to get mastery over him, once more resumes the struggle and endeavours to bring him back to worldly life, and how Māra is again ignominiously defeated.

The two last ballads are also found in the Mahāvastu where we also meet with a ballad on the birth of Buddha. In the Mahāparinibbānasutta again, some of the verses are certainly remnants of ballads on the passing away of the Master not (as Bishop Copleston thought) taken from a Buddha epic. And again in the Lalitavistara the oldest and

[1] Sacred Books of the East, Vol. 10 (II), p. 124.

most valuable parts are ballads on the most momentous episodes in the life of the Buddha. It is on such ballads as those found in the Lalitavistara that the first real *epic* treating of the life of Buddha, *Aśvaghoṣa's Buddha Carita*, was based.

Once more in Buddhistic literature we can observe the transition from ballad poetry to the epic in the case of the Dipavaṁśa and Mahāvaṃśa. The former contains old ballads on legendary history of Buddhism in Ceylon, while the Mahāvaṃśa treats the same matter in the form of a perfect epic, a Mahākāvya.

But not only the life of Buddha has been the subject of ballads. We find also a great many other legends in form of ballads in different parts of the Tripiṭaka. A regular ballad in prose and verse is the legend of the robber Aṅgulimāla who became a monk and rose to be an Arhat, in the Majjhima-nikāya (86). Here (Nr. 83) we find also the ballad of king Makhādeva who, at the appearance of his first grey hair gives up his kingdom and enters the order of monks. One of the most beautiful of these ballads is found in the Raṭṭhapālasutta (Nr. 82), of which I will read you a short abstract.

Young prince Raṭṭhapāla desires to become a monk. His parents absolutely refuse to consent, but through abstaining from taking any food he compels them to give their permission. Years pass, and one day he returns as a monk, to his native town and begs at the door of his parents' home. His father does not recognise him and turns him away from the threshold with angry words of abuse. "By these shaven monks," he cries, our only dearly beloved son was induced to renounce the world." Meanwhile the nurse comes out to throw away some scraps of food. The mendicant begs for these scraps for his meal. While he eats them the old nurse recognises him as the son of the house, and informs her master of it. The latter comes and invites his son to enter the house. Raṭṭhapāla politely declines by saying, "No, I have already dined to-day." But he accepts an invitation for the next day. And his father prepares not only a meal for him, but heaps of gold and jewellery in the dining room and instructs the former wives of Raṭṭhapāla to put on all their ornaments. On the next day he is received splendidly and his father offers him all the jewels and treasures. But Raṭṭhapāla only says: "If you will follow my advice, father, then load all this gold and ornaments on a cart and throw it into the Ganges where it is deepest. And why? Because only pain and misery, wretchedness and suffering will arise out of it." Nor will he have anything to do with the women who throw themselves coaxingly at his feet. After he has finished his meal, he quietly departs. Then he meets the king of the Kuru land and has a conversation with him. The king says, he could understand why a person who has become old or ill or poor or has lost his relatives should become a monk, but he could never understand, why one who is young and happy and in good health, should renounce the world. Raṭṭhapāla answers him with a discourse on the vanity of existence and the insatiableness of desire and convinces the king in a magnificent dialogue of the truth of the Buddha doctrine.

Some of the most beautiful Buddhist ballads occur in the Saṃyuttanikāya. Especially in the Mārasaṁyutta and the Bhikkhumsamyutta we find some of the best specimens of the oldest Buddhist poetry. Some of the short ballads found in the chapter on Māra and the nuns are among the finest productions of ancient Indian poetic art. Let me read to you only one of these ballads (5. 3) in a translation that of the nun Kisā-Gotamī (Gotamī the slender one):

Thus I have heard. The Master once sojourned at Sāvatthi in the Jetagrove in the garden of Anāthapiṇḍaka. The nun Kisā-Gotamī, after having put her robes on went in the morning into the town of Sāvatthi, with her alms-bowl under her garment, to beg for food. And after she had been begging in Sāvatthi and had returned with the food which she had obtained by begging she went after her meal, into the dark forest, in order to spend the day there. Then, when she had retired far into the dark forest, and sat down at the foot of a tree, to stay there for the day,—

Then Māra, the Evil One, desiring to cause fear, terror and horror to the nun Kisā-Gotamī and to disturb her deep meditation, went to the place where the nun Kisā-Gotamī was. And after having come near her, he addressed to the nun Kisā-Gotamī the verse:

"Why sittest thou, so lonesome there,
Like to a mother who has lost her son,
With tearful face, alone in the deep forest
Is it a man thou seekest?"

Then the nun Kisā-Gotamī thought to herself, "Who is it, a human or a non-human being, who uttered a verse just now?" and it occurred to the nun Kisā-Gotamī:

"It is Māra the Evil One, who in order to cause fear, terror and horror to me and to disturb my deep meditation has uttered the verse." But when the nun Kisā-Gotamī knew that it was Māra, the Evil One, she addressed Māra, the Evil One, in the following verse:

"I am indeed a mother who has lost her son,
But men who would be near enough I need not seek,
I do not mourn nor weep,
Nor have I any fear of thee, my friend.
For lust is quite destroyed in me,
Dense darkness torn away;
Death's army I have conquered, and I live from all evil free."

Then Māra, the Evil One, knew that the nun Kisā-Gotamī had recognised him, and unhappy and in low spirits he vanished from the spot.

Many more such ballads are found in the Jātaka Gāthās, and again in the Thera and Therīgāthās.

An extremely dramatic ballad is that of Sundarī in Therīgāthā (312-327):

In amazement the Brāhman Sujāta asks his wife Vasiṭṭhī how it is that she does not weep, though she has lost her seven children, when formerly she used to weep night and day for her deceased babes. She replies, that she has learnt from the Buddha how to escape birth and death :

> "Nay, Brahmin, many hundreds of our babes,
> And of our kinsfolk many hundred more,
> Have we in all the ages past and gone
> Seen preyed upon by death, both you and I.
> But I have learnt how from both birth and death
> A way there is t'escape, wherefore no more
> I mourn, nor weep, nor make any bitter wail."

Then the Brahmin too goes to Buddha and becomes a monk. He sends his charioteer back with a message to his wife that he has renounced the world. The woman is about to give the charioteer a horse and carriage and a thousand pieces of gold for the good news. But he replies :

> "Let them remain thine own, O Brahminee,
> Horses and chariots and the thousand coins,
> For I too, have a mind to leave the world,
> Near him of chiefest wisdom to abide."

Thereupon she offers to make her daughter Sundarī the heir of her father's estate. But Sundarī, too, rejecting cattle and horses, elephants, jewels and rings and all her father's estate, has made up her mind to renounce this world. And her mother wishes her success. And Sujātā becomes a great Therī and she is said to be the author of the poem.

Perhaps the most beautiful of these ballads is that of Śubhā, the nun whom a gallant tries to seduce, who plucks out her eye which the man has admired so much (Therīgatha 366 ff.) :[1]

> " In Jīvaka's pleasant woodland walked Śubhā
> The Bhikkunī. A gallant met her there

[1] Translated by Mr. Rhys Davids, p. 149 (abridged).

And barred the way. To him thus spake Śubhā :
'What have I done to offend thee, that thus in my path thou comest?
No man, O friend, it beseemeth to touch
a sister in orders?
... ......Why standest thou blocking my pathway?
Me pure, thou impure of heart, me passionless, thou of vile passions ;
Me who as to the whole of me freed am in spirit and blameless,
Me whence comes it that thou dost hinder, standing obnoxious?'
'Young art thou ; maiden, and faultless—what seekest thou in the holy life?
Cast off that yellow-hued raiment and come! in the blossoming wood-land
Seek we our pleasure. Filled with the incense of blossoms the trees waft
Sweetness. See, the springs at the prime the season of happiness!
Come with me then to the flowering wood-land and seek we our pleasure
Haunted is the great forest with many a herd of wild creatures,
Broken its peace by the trampling of elephants rutting and savage.
Empty of mankind and fearsome—is't there thou would'st go uncompanioned?
Thou like a gold wrought statue like nymph in celestial garden
Movest, O peerless creature. Radiant would shine thy loveliness
Robed in raiment of beauty, diaphanous gear of Benares.................
Dearer and sweeter to me than art thou in the world is no creature,
Thou with the languid and slow moving eyes of an elf of the forest.
If thou wilt list to me, come where the joys of the sheltered life wait thee,
Dwell in a house of Verandas and terraces, hand-maidens serving thee.
Robe thyself in delicate gear of Benares, don garlands, use unguents...'
'What now to thee, in this carrion-filled grave-filling carcase so fragile
Seen by thee, seemeth to warrant the doctrine thou speakest infatuate?'
'Eyes hast thou like the gazelle's, like an elf's in the heart of the mountains
'Tis those eyes of thee, sight of which feedeth the depth of my passion...
Though thou be far from me, how could I ever forget thee, O maiden,
Thee of the long-drawn eye-lashes, thee of the eyes so miraculous?
Dearer to me than those orbs is naught, O thou witching-eyed fairy!'
'Lo, thou art wanting to walk where no path is, thou seekest to capture
Moon from the skies for thy play, thou would'st jump o'er the ridges of Meru,
Thou who presumest to lie in wait for a child of the Buddha.

Nowhere in earth or in heaven lives now any object of lust for me......
Tempt thou some women who hath not discerned what I say, or whose teacher
Is but a learner; haply she'll listen; tempt thou not Śubhā;
She understandeth. And now 'tis thyself hast vexation and failure......
Oh, I have seen it—a puppet well-painted, with new wooden spindles,
Cunningly fastened with strings and with pins, and diversely dancing.
But if the strings and the pins be all drawn out and loosened and scattered,
So that the puppet be made non-existent and broken in pieces,
Which of the parts wilt thou choose and appoint for my heart's rest and solace
Such is the manner wherein persist these poor little bodies.
Take away members and attributes—nothing disturbeth in any wise......
What is this eye but a little ball lodged in the fork of a hollow tree,
Bubble of film, anointed with tearbrine, exuding slime-drops,
Compost wrought in the shape of an eye of manifold aspect?'
Forthwith the maiden so lovely tore out her eye and gave it to him:
'Here, then! take thou thine eye!' Nor sinned she, her heart unobstructed.
Straightway the lust in him ceased and he her pardon imploring:
'O that thou mightest recover thy sight, thou maid pure and holy!
Never again will I dare to offend thee after this fashion.
Sore hast thou smitten my sin, blazing flames have I clasped to my bosom;
Poisonous snake have I handled—but O! be thou healed and forgive me!'
Freed from molesting, the Bhikkhunī went on her way to the Buddha,
Chief of th' awakened. There in his presence, seeing those features
Born of uttermost merit, straightway her sight was restored to her."

These ballads have all the dialogue form, and generally the dialogue is sufficient to make the hearer understand the course of the narrative. Where this was not the case, brief prose formulas, a short introduction, and a few short sentences in prose were inserted. The next step in the development of the ballad was that narrative stanzas were inserted between the stanzas containing the conversation. This last stage is mostly represented in these Buddhist ballads; and they form the bridge to the epic.

But all these Buddhist ballads are also full of dramatic movement, and some scholars are inclined to see in them real 'little dramas.' But it is not likely that any dramatic performance was connected with them. For in the whole Tripiṭaka we do not find any trace of sacred dramas being performed. On the contrary, the Buddhist monks were forbidden to take part in any plays or dramatic performances. In the time of Aśvaghoṣa, it is true, this rule was no longer observed. For Aśvaghoṣa himself is the author of a Buddhist drama, fragments of which have been discovered in Turfan (Central Asia).

There is certainly a strong dramatic element in all these ballads, both secular and religious. And there can be no doubt, that they contributed as much to the *origin of the drama* as to the origin of the epic.

Indian writers on poetics have often said that the *drama* is the highest form of poetry; and in the West also the drama is generally considered to be the highest type of poetic production. The reason for this estimate is, that in the drama epic and lyric poetry are combined with imitative representation of life *to one* harmonious work of art. And this combination of literary arts is not only the highest perfection but also (though only in a rudimentary form) the *beginning* of poetic art. For in *one* sense the drama is the first of all kinds of poetry. Primitive people, like children will never tell a story, without accompanying it with corresponding gestures. Among the Australian natives and other primitive people we find very artistic pantomimes. But even among civilised peoples it was impossible in ancient time to make a ballad known to the public, except by recitation accompanied by pantomime. Thus in the ballad there is always a strong dramatic element. And an American scholar (G. Morey Miller[1] in the

[1] The Dramatic Element in Popular Ballad.

University Studies of the University of Cincinnati 1905) has proved from a comparison of the ballad poetry of numerous peoples, that the recitation of ballads was originally always combined with song and dramatic dance. It is well known to ethnologists that dance among primitive people is always mimic dance, representing some action and that this dance is closely connected with the origin of the drama. The ancient or primitive ballads themselves are so dramatic that Morey Miller calls them 'Ballad plays.'

Now in India also we have found a rich literature of ballads first in the dialogue hymns of the Ṛgveda, then in the Ākhyānas and Itihāsas embodied in the Mahābhārata and in some of the Purāṇas and again in old Buddhist literature and some of the Jaina sacred texts. All these ballads which chiefly consist of dialogues, are very dramatic and some Western scholars are now inclined to see in them real dramas.

The fact is that in India to the present day there is no sharp line of demarcation between ballad recitation and the dramatic performance. When Sir George Grierson had read my account of the Buddhist ballads, he wrote to me (in 1912), that these ballads reminded him of the *Khyals* of Rājasthān, written in Mārwarī dialect. These Khyals treat some popular legend in the form of a dialogue in verses, or a prose tale mixed with dialogue verses, and they are sometimes recited by one person only, and sometimes acted on the stage. And what you here in Bengal hear and see at *Yātrā* productions and *Kirtans* may be called recitation as well as drama. K. Ramavarma Raja (J. R. A. S. 1910) describes the Dramas (as he calls them), produced by the Cakkyars in Mālabār whom he describes as the representatives of Paurāṇic Sutas, and his whole description shows, that he does not make any distinction between recitation and dramatic performance. Even in Sanskrit such expressions as *bharata* and *kuśīlava* are used both for singers and bards, and for actors.

This, however, is only a survival of an early stage of poetry, when our distinctions between epic, lyric and dramatic poetry cannot be applied at all, but when all poetry was dramatic, epic and lyric at the same time and generally accompanied by dancing, music and singing.

And we may add : this poetry was as a rule religious. In India also, the oldest ballads were those in which stories of divine or half-divine beings were told and which were recited at sacrifices and festivals. And as in other countries, in India also the drama is deeply rooted in the religious cult. Many of the ancient Vedic ceremonies as described in the Śrautasūtras, are almost dramatic performances, at which priests and sacrificers are the actors. In post-Vedic times plays were connected with the Indradhvaja festival at the end of the rainy season, and especially with the cult of the gods Viṣṇu (both as Rāma and Kṛṣṇa) and Śiva. The Viṣṇu Purāṇa describes how the Gopīs, allured by the songs of Kṛṣṇa and Balarāma at night gather around the god, to perform the Rāsa dance, and how dancing they imitate the deeds and adventures of Kṛṣṇa.

That dancing and acting are closely connected is proved by the terms Nāṭaka, Naṭa, Nāṭya, Naṭyati which are all connected with the Prakrit root Naṭ, Nṛt 'to dance.'

Traces of the religious origin of the Sanskrit drama are still to be found in our literary dramas which all begin with a Nandi, an introductory prayer.

This Nandi, however, is only a remnant of a longer religious ceremony, the Pūrvaranga, which is described in the Bharatīya-Nāṭyaśāstra. This Pūrvaranga preceded the production of every play and consisted of invocation of the deities with music, singing and dancing.

The religious origin of the Indian drama has also left its trace in the fact, that myths and legends especially those of Rāma and Kṛṣṇa, have in all centuries been the favourite subjects of the drama and even Buddhist poets made scenes from the Buddha legend the subject of their plays. And the popular dramatic performances in modern India are still a religious affair such as the Yātrās in Bengal, the Bhavais in Gujrat, and the Swang in the Punjab.

But this ancient ballad poetry in its connection with minor dances at religious festivals, it must be remembered, is only one of the sources of the Indian drama. There must also have existed in ancient India some sort of popular plays in which scenes from real life were represented for the entertainment of the people. We have no direct proof of the existence of such plays, but we hear already in later Vedic texts and still more in the epic and Buddhist texts of Naṭas, a low class of itinerant players or 'actors.' The popular plays, produced by these Naṭas, were probably not literary works but improvisations which were never written down. But the poets who created the literary drama, had seen such popular performances, and imitated them in a refined form.

In the different kinds of dramatic poetry, and in the peculiarities of the Indian classical drama we find traces both of ancient religious ballad and of the coarse popular play. The connection with the ancient ballad poetry is more conspicuous in the Nāṭaka, while the influence of the popular play is more visible in the *Prakaraṇa*.

The Vyāyoga of which the Madhyamavyāyoga, one of the plays ascribed to Bhāsa, is a good example, is little more than a dramatised ballad. And if the plays ascribed to Bhāsa are really the works of this poet, all those dramas of his which are based on Mahābhārata stories or on the Kṛṣṇa and the Rāma legends, clearly betray their origin from the ancient heroic ballad. But about this question—the authorship of 'Bhāsa's plays'—I shall have to speak in my next lecture.[1]

M. Winternitz

[1] Lecture delivered at the Calcutta University on 20th August, 1923.

# INDIAN LITERATURE AND WORLD-LITERATURE

The word 'world-literature' may be used in two different meanings. In the great *national* literatures of the world we find some works which have become the common property of all nations. The Hebrew Bible and the New Testament, the poems of Homer, the fables of Æsop, the Arabian Nights, the plays of Shakespeare—to mention only some of the best known examples—belong to 'world-literature' in this sense. These are works that are read, enjoyed and appreciated by so many nations, that we can say, they belong to civilised mankind, to the literature of the world. But we also speak of 'world-literature,' as distinguished from the national literatures, when by a comparative study of the literatures of different nations we try to trace the mutual relations between them, the influences exercised by one literature upon another. When we use 'world-literature' in this sense, we mean to say, that the object of our study is not one particular literature, but the literature of the world, and we wish to find out, what part each nation has played in it, and what each of them has contributed to the common stock of ideas, thoughts, poetical motives and literary treasures.

I shall have to use 'world-literature' in both these senses, when I try to answer the questions: What has India contributed to the literature of the world? In which way has Indian literature influenced other literatures, and what impulses has it received from the literatures of other nations?

In the year 1808 a little book was published in Germany with the title: 'Die Sprache und Weisheit der Indier' ("The Language and Wisdom of the Indians") by the poet

Friedrich Schlegel, who by this book became the pioneer of Indian Philology in Germany. This little book was written with enthusiasm and inspired enthusiasm. And ever since then it has become the custom in Germany to speak of the 'wisdom of India' or of 'Indian wisdom.' And what is generally meant by this 'wisdom' are on the whole the ideas and thoughts found in the Upaniṣads, in the Bhagavadgītā and in the sacred books of the Buddhists.

It is the Upaniṣads which we have first to mention as Indian works belonging to world-literature. Long before a scholarly study of the Upaniṣads began in Europe, the mystic doctrines of the Upaniṣads had influenced Western thought in many a way. Persian Sufism has received impulses from these doctrines, and it is at least probable that the mystic-theosophical Logos doctrine of the Neo-Platonic School and of the Alexandrian Christians and even the teachings of the Christian mystics Eckhart and Tauler were in some way or other influenced by the Atman-Brahman doctrine of the Upaniṣads. But if it is possible, that in some of these cases we have to see rather a parallel development, than any direct or indirect influences, there can be no doubt that the philosophy of the great German mystic of the nineteenth century, Schopenhauer, was greatly impressed with the teaching of the Upaniṣads. In the 17th century Dara Shikoh, the unfortunate brother of the Emperor Aurangzeb, the son of Shah Jehan, had a collection of Upaniṣads translated into Persian. At the very beginning of the 19th century the French scholar Anquetil Duperron, who was not only a great admirer of Indian thought, but actually lived like an Indian ascetic, translated the Upaniṣads from the Persian of Dara Shikoh into Latin. This imperfect and often faulty translation with the title 'Oupnekhat' was yet read and studied with the greatest enthusiasm by the German Philosopher Schopenhauer who called it "the production of highest human wisdom" (die Ausgeburt der höchsten menschlichen Weisheit). Schopenhauer calls

Plato, Kant and the 'Vedas' (by this he means the Upaniṣads) his teachers. The harmony between his own system and that of the Upaniṣads seemed to him quite marvellous. The book 'Oupnekhat' was always lying open on his table. And he says of this book: "It is the most profitable and elevating reading that (with the exception of the original text) is possible in the world; it has been the solace of my life and will be that of my death." But the fundamental teaching of the Upaniṣads is the same which, in the words of Schopenhauer, "was at all times the laughing-stock of the fools and the object of endless meditation of the wise," namely the *doctrine of unity*, that is to say, the doctrine, "that all manifoldness is only apparent, that in all the individuals of this world in whatever endless number they may present themselves after and beside one another, there manifests itself only one and the same truly existing Being that is present in and identical with all of them."

Yet I believe, it is a wild exaggeration when Schopenhauer says that the teaching of the Upaniṣads represents "the fruit of the highest human knowledge and wisdom" and contains "almost superhuman conceptions the originators of which can hardly be regarded as mere mortals," or when Deussen, one of the foremost followers of Schopenhauer, says that these thinkers have acquired "if not the most scientific, yet the most intimate and direct information on the last secret of all being."

Philosophy means "love of wisdom" and the greater philosopher is, in my opinion, not he who fancies himself to be in possession of highest wisdom, but he who *loves truth* above everything else and strives to approach it as far as it is possible for human beings. It is true philosophy when the Bṛhadāraṇyaka-Upaniṣad says that the last principle, the Brahman or the Atman, can only be described by *neti neti* ("No, no" or "it is not so," "it is not so"). The philosopher poets of the Upaniṣads will always be admired and esteemed in the East and in the West, not because they have *found* the truth, but because they have *struggled* so earnestly for truth, because in their philosophical poetry the eternally unsatiated human *longing* for knowledge has found such fervent expression. What makes the Upaniṣads so extremely valuable for us, is not that they contain "*superhuman* conceptions," but rather that they contain *human*, entirely human *attempts* at coming as near the truth as possible. And in this sense they will always keep a prominent place in the literature of the world and in the history of human thought.

The Bhagavadgītā also belongs to world-literature. The English translation of the poem by Charles Wilkins, published in 1785, was the first Sanskrit book that was directly translated from Sanskrit into an European language. In a letter to Nathaniel Smith, printed in this translation, Warren Hastings writes, that such writings as the Bhagavadgītā "will survive when the British dominion in India shall have long ceased to exist, and when the sources which it once yielded of wealth and power are lost to remembrance."

In 1823, August Wilhelm von Schlegel (who was the first Professor of Sanskrit in Germany, being in 1818 called to the newly founded University of Bonn)—published the first critical edition of the text with a Latin translation. This work attracted the attention of the great German writer Wilhelm von Humboldt. He read the poem with great enthusiasm, wrote a lengthy essay on it, and praised it as "the profoundest and loftiest thing the world has ever seen." And in a letter to a friend he wrote, that when he read the poem for the first time, he had a constant feeling of gratitude to Providence that it had allowed him to live long enough to become acquainted with this work. It has been repeatedly translated into German, as well as into English, and also there are translations into other European languages.

Christian readers of the Bhagavadgītā have always been struck by the resemblances between the *Bhakti* doctrine proclaimed in the Gītā, and Christian ideas. And there have been scholars who tried to prove that the Bhagavadgītā was influenced by Christian views, and that its author was acquainted with the New Testament. Thus Lorinser (in the appendix to his German translation, 1869) has pointed out more than 100 parallel passages to the Gospels in the Bhagavadgītā. But if we go through these passages, we shall find that there are hardly twenty-five passages, where the similarity is great enough to allow us to think even of the possibility of a borrowing, and there is no case in which the assumption of borrowing is more probable than that of accidental agreement. And with the exception of E. W. Hopkins I do not know of any scholar who believes in Christian influence on the Bhagavadgītā. It seems that the Bhakti doctrine is as old as Pāṇini. And we know from an inscription on a stone column found at Besnagar near Bhilsa in the Gwalior State, that in the 2nd century B. C. even a Greek, Heliodorus, son of Dion, a native of Taxila, had adopted the Bhāgavata faith. The coincidences between the Bhagavadgītā and the Christian Gospels, as far as there are any, must, therefore, be explained as an interesting case of parallel development of religious ideas, without any mutual influencing.

It was under the influence of the Bhakti doctrine of the Bhagavadgītā, and not under Christian influence, as Father J. Dahlmann would have us believe, that the Mahāyāna Buddhism was developed. For there is no proof of Christian influence in India before the 2nd and 3rd century A. D. And the Mahāyāna is certainly older.

The relation between Buddhism and Christianity, Buddhist and Christian literature, has been the subject of much discussion. As Buddhism has become a world-religion, so many parts of *Buddhist literature* belong to world-literature.

Much has been written about the parallels between the Buddha legend and the legend of Christ, and coincidences between sayings, parables and similes of Buddhist sacred texts, and those found in the Gospels, and it has often been asserted, that the Christian Gospels were largely influenced by the Buddhist Tipiṭaka, both as regards the legends and the teaching. But both the real and the apparent parallels have been greatly exaggerated. A most careful and detailed comparison of the two bodies of texts shows most clearly that the differences are infinitely greater than the coincidences, and that there is no *certain* case of borrowing on the part of the Christian Gospels. There are only a few cases in which mutual influence can be admitted as being *possible*, and only very few cases, in which such influence is *probable*. There is, for instance, the legend of Asita who comes to see the infant Buddha, and prophesies his future greatness, which bears a strong similarity to the legend of Simeon in the Gospel of Luke. As the Buddhist legend occurs already in an old ballad of the Suttanipāta and was known in the third century B. C., it is not improbable that the Christian legend is borrowed from Buddhist tradition. There may be three or four other cases where a historical connexion between Buddhist and Christian legends is possible or even probable.

Single utterances and parables of Jesus and of the Buddha have also often been compared, but in all these cases it is only a matter of distant resemblance, or of such general ideas as could easily occur and actually do occur in the sacred books of all religions.

A careful comparison of the Buddhist sacred texts and the Christian Gospels does not lead us to believe in any *direct* influence of the Buddhist *literature* on the Gospels. On the other hand it is certain, that ever since the times of Alexander the Great there existed the possibility of Buddhist ideas being infused into Western minds. And it is at all events possible that in that combination of Jewish and Greek ideas on which the teaching of the Christian Gospels is based, there was also a small admixture of Buddhist thoughts and legends.

But it is not before the 2nd and 3rd centuries A.D. that we have certain proofs of a knowledge of Buddhism in the West. And this is also the time when the *Apocryphal Gospels* were composed, in which we find some undoubted borrowings from Buddhist literature.

But the influence of Buddhist literature on the West became far more apparent in later times. One of the most popular books in all Christian countries during the whole of the middle ages was the *Book of Barlaam and Joasaph*, and there can be not the least doubt, that this work was composed by a pious Christian monk who knew the Buddha legend from some Indian source, probably from the Lalitavistara. For the frame story of this famous Christian novel is nothing else but the Buddha legend with all its principal features, and some of the parables inserted in the book are well known in Indian literature. The work was probably first composed in the Pehlevi language in the 6th or 7th century A.D., and afterwards translated into Arabic and Syrian. From the Syrian text probably the Greek version was derived, which was translated into Latin. The Latin translation then became the source of numerous translations into almost all European languages. In time Barlaam and Joasaph became so familiar figures among Christian people, that they were looked upon as pious Christian men, who had actually lived and preached, and were finally included in the catalogue of Christian saints by the Roman Catholic Church. But Joasaph is nothing else, but *Judasaf* which is a misreading of *Budasaph* (in Arabic, Syrian and Pehlevi *j* and *b* are very similar), that is Bodhisattva. Thus it came about that the Bodhisattva has become a Christian saint. (In the *Catalogus Sanctorum* of Peter de Natalibus, 1370, Barlaam and Joasaph appear already as saints.)

And as in the Middle Ages, so has the Indian Buddha legend shown a wonderful vitality over and over again down to our own times. In the 19th century, the epic poem, 'The Light of Asia,' describing the career of the Buddha, of the

English poet Edwin Arnold met with such an enthusiasm, that more than 60 editions of the book were published in England, and more than a hundred in America.

Again in 1906 the Danish poet Karl Gjellerup who has some years ago been distinguished by the Nobel prize, has written his beautiful novel 'The Pilgrim Kamanita,' which is entirely inspired by Buddhist ideas, and by the Mahāyāna accounts of the paradise Sukhavati. Even more than the ideas of the Upaniṣads and of the Bhagavadgītā, Buddhist ideas have exercised and are still exercising an enormous influence on western thought.

The Bhagavadgītā is an episode of the Mahābhārata. There are at least two more episodes of the great Epic which have become part of the world literature: The *Nalopākhyāna* and the *Sāvitry-upākhyāna*.

The story of Nala and Damayanti is one of the best known Indian poems in Europe. Ever since Franz Bopp first published the Sanskrit text of the story with a Latin translation in the year 1819, it has been considered as one of the gems of the poetry of the world. It has been translated into nearly all European languages; and in the Western Universities it has become an almost general custom, to begin the study of Sanskrit with reading the story of Nala. It was the first Sanskrit book which I myself read about forty years ago, and I shall never forget the spell it exercised upon me, and the enthusiasm with which I read it from canto to canto.

The wonderful story of Sāvitrī, too, that ideal woman, who by her faithfulness and love and by her wisdom and strength conquers Death, has been translated into European languages and has always been highly appreciated in the West. I know of seven translations into German, and I have seen it on the stage, turned into an opera and set to music, in our German theatre at Prague.

There is also the famous parable in the Strīparvan of the Mahābhārata, the parable of *the Man in the Well,* which has become part of the literature of the world. It is the parable of the Brahman who loses his way in a terrible forest with horrible dragons, etc., falls into a well, remains hanging in the branches of a creeper, sees a mighty serpent in the middle of the well, a giant elephant at the top, but seeing honey dripping down from the branches of the tree, he greedily swallows it, as he is not weary of existence. The parable is meant to illustrate the saṃsāra with all its evils and dangers, and man who inspite of all continues to enjoy sensual pleasures. This parable was included in the book of Barlaam and Joasaph and in the Kalilag and Damnag, and has wandered all over the world. The Persian Sufi poet Jelal-ed-Din Rūmi translated it into Persian from which Ruckert rendered it into German in a poem which is known to every child in Germany. It has equally served for the edification of Brahmans, Buddhists and Jains, as of Jews, Mahomedans and Christians.

When we come to classical literature, Kālidāsa certainly takes his place in world-literature, by the side of Shakespeare. His 'Śakuntalā' was translated into English by Sir William Jones in 1789, and when it was soon after (1791) translated from English into German by Georg Forster, it roused at once an enthusiasm among literary people all over Europe and more especially in Germany, which we can hardly understand to-day. It was looked upon like a wonder, coming from "the land of wonders" and was hailed by men like Herder and Goethe with surprise and delight. Herder wrote a lengthy essay in form of letters on the drama, and Goethe, immediately after he had read Forster's translation, wrote his well known verses in which he expressed his enthusiastic admiration for 'Śakuntalā.' And almost half a century later, in 1830, as an old man, Goethe wrote in a letter to the French editor of the Sanskrit text of 'Śakuntalā' Chézy, in which he says: "The first time when I became aware of this unfathomable work, it excited such an enthusiasm in me and attracted me so much, that I never left off studying it, and even felt myself urged on to the impossible task of adapting it, at least in some way, to the German stage." Schiller also wrote to Goethe in a letter, that he had been thinking of making use of the 'Śakuntalā' for the theatre, but had to give up the idea, as it was too delicate for the stage.

Nevertheless several attempts have been made to adapt the drama to the stage in Europe, and several versions have been produced in German theatres. In Paris it was brought on the stage in form of a ballet. In England it was first produced in 1899 (in the translation of Monier Williams), and again in 1912 and 1913.

The *Vikramorvaśīya* also has been translated into European languages, and it was also produced on the stage in 1888 as an opera (Urvaśī) in Munich. And again the *Mālavikāgnimitra* has been not only translated but also adapted for the stage and a version of it was produced at the Munich theatre in 1917 only.

There is only one other Indian drama that has been translated repeatedly and adapted for the stage, the *Mṛcchakaṭika* of king Śūdraka. In Paris it was produced in 1850 and in another adaptation in 1895. In Germany one adaptation of *Mṛcchakaṭika* has attracted large audiences to the theatres about 1892-93 and more recently again—only two or three years ago—another version was produced at Dresden and Leipzig. At the latter place I saw it myself in 1921.

But no work of Indian literature belongs so truly to the literature of the world as the *Pañcatantra.* It is one of the most fascinating study in the history of world-literature to follow up the traces by which Indian stories and motives of stories have wandered from nation to nation, so that we meet with them amongst all peoples of Asia and Europe, nay even among Somalis and Suahilis on the African coast. Not only have single Indian tales been spread to other peoples by travellers, merchants, and itinerant monks, but even whole Indian *books* of stories and fables have become the common property of many peoples. The most prominent of these books is the *Pañcatantra*, and when Theodor Benfey in the epoch-making introduction to his German translation of the *Pañcatantra* (1859), with his astounding knowledge of Eastern and Western languages and literatures, traced the history of the *Pañcatantra* on its wanderings through the world-literature, he laid the foundation of what has since been termed 'Comparative History of Literature,' and has become a new branch of historical and literary research. The translations of the Pañcatantra into Eastern and Western languages go back to a very early time. Already in the 6th century A. D., the fame of the *Pañcatantra* had reached Persia. For a North-West Indian recension of the work was translated into Pehlevi by the Physician Burzoe on the order of the Persian king Khosrau Anosherwan (531-579 A. D.), together with some other Indian stories. This Pehlevi translation has not been preserved, but we can reconstruct it with the help of an old Syrian and an old Arabian translation, derived from the Pehlevi text. Already about 570 A. D. the Syrian Christian monk Bud translated it from the Pehlevi into Syrian under the title '*Kalilag and Damnag*.' This translation has come down to us only in a fragmentary form. But about 750 Abdalla ibn al-Moqaffa translated the same Pehlevi text into Arabic, with some additions of his own, under the title 'Kalila wa Dimna.' (Kalila and Dimna or Kalilag and Damnag in Syrian are corruptions of the names करटक and दमनक of the two jackals in the first book of the *Pañcatantra*).

This Arabic translation has become the source of so many translations into European and Asiatic languages, that the German translator of this Arabic version, Ph. Wolff could justly say of it, that 'next to the Bible it had been translated into most languages of the world,' and that he called it a book, that 'had inspired whole nations, and to which kings and princes paid attention and honour.' But the Pehlevi work consisted not only of the five books of the Pañcatantra, but of several more books, in which some moral tales of the Mahābhārata and some Buddhist stories were translated.

The Arabic translation of this book was translated into Greek in the 11th century and from Greek into Italian, Latin, German, and Slavonic languages. At the beginning of the 12th century it was translated into Hebrew by Rabbi Joël and between 1263-1278 from Hebrew into Latin by the baptised Jew John of Capua. A German translation of this Latin version was among the first printed books, and has exercised enormous influence on German literature and was translated again into many other European languages.

By an almost bewildering number of channels the stories of the Pañcatantra have travelled all over the East and the West, and translations of the work have become some of the most popular books in Europe during the Middle Ages. Hence it is no wonder, that we find traces of Indian fables and tales in the most popular narrative works of western literature, such as the 'Gesta Romanorum' and similar collections of monks' tales in Latin, in the French fabliaux, in the works of the famous story-tellers Boccaccio and Straparola in Italy, of Chaucer in England and Lafontaine in France, and even in the German 'Household Tales' collected by the brothers Grimm.

The unity of East and West is nowhere so clearly demonstrated as in the history of *Pañcatantra*.

Other Indian story books that have contributed much to the narrative literature of the world, are the *Vetāla-pañcaviṃśatikā* which has been translated into Hindi and other vernaculars, from Hindi into English and German, and part of which is included in the Mongolian story book 'Siddikür'; the *Vikramacarita* (or *Siṃhāsanadvātriṃśika*) which was translated into Persian about 1574 by order of Emperor Akbar, and a Mongolian version of which is known by the title "The Story of Ardshi Bordshi Khan"; and the *Śukasaptati*, 'The

70 stories of the Parrot,' which by its Persian and Turkish translations known as the *Tūtināmeh* ('The Parrot Book'), has exercised great influence on the literatures of the West.

When Benfey, in his famous introduction to the Pañcatantra, was able to prove that the sources of numerous Western stories were to be found in India, he was carried along by the enthusiasm, so common to pioneers, to assert that India was the home of *all* fairy tales and stories. Nobody would accept this theory to-day, for we know that there cannot be one place of origin for all stories and tales in the world. Just as imagination is the common property of men, thus the love of hearing and telling stories is generally human, and there is no people, however primitive, where we do not find some stories and fairy tales. But this very love of story-telling, which is common to all peoples, is the cause, why all peoples are inclined to listen to foreign tales, and tell them again as their own. And it may well be, that in the great exchange of stories between the peoples, one people may have to give more than the other. This seems to be the case with India. Though we do no longer believe with Benfey, that India is the home of *all* tales, it yet remains true, that numerous stories current all over the world can be traced back to Indian sources.

It is even highly probable that two famous books of the world-literature, the book of Sindbad and the Arabian Nights are at least partly of Indian origin. The '*Book of Sindbad*' is known in an Arabic, a Persian, a Syrian, a Hebrew and a Greek version. The Arabic version is also included in the 'Arabian Nights' with the title 'The Seven Veziers,' and in Europe there is quite a number of popular books known by the name of 'The Seven Sages.' The Arabian writer Masudi (who died 956 A. D.) says that the Kitab es-Sindbad was derived from an Indian book. This Indian book has not yet been discovered, yet it is highly probable that there was such an Indian source of the

'Sindbad.' For the introduction is very similar to that of the *Pañcatantra*. In the Sindbad, too, a king hands his sons over to a sage who promises to instruct them within six months in such a way, 'that no wiser man should be found in the whole country.' The stories are, as in the *Pañcatantra* and other Indian narrative works, included in a frame story, and they are told to save the life of a prince who is condemned to death. This also is an Indian idea. Most of the stories are actually found in one or other of the Indian narrative works. As the principal subject of the work (as in the *Śukasaptati*) is the wickedness of women, it is not unlikely that it was intended to be a kind of supplement to the Pañcatantra, a book of instruction for princes to warn them against the wiles of women.

The 'Arabian Nights' also are believed by some scholars to be of Indian origin. This is not probable. But certain it is that this famous book of the world-literature shows marked Indian influences. In a Jaina commentary of the 11th century we find a number of tales encased in a frame story of the queen Kaṇayamanjarī who tells stories in a similar way as Sheherezade in the 'Arabian Nights.' And it has been proved that all the essential motives of the frame story of the 'Arabian Nights' are Indian. It is probable enough that the Persian author of the tales composed the frame story and a number of tales in imitation of Indian originals, but the bulk of the tales is not Indian.

When we can trace stories through actual translations of works such as the *Pañcatantra* or the *Śukasaptati* we are on the safe ground of facts. In other cases, when we find the same stories in Indian and other literatures, it can only be decided with more or less probability, whether India's has been the giving or the taking part. And often it is impossible to decide at all.

Thus, it is a much discussed question whether the *fables*, which Indian and Greek literature have in common, are Indian or Greek in their origin. The question cannot be decided by chronological arguments, for only a few Greek fables can be dated, and the so-called 'fables of Æsop' belong to different times. It is true, that the Greek beast fable goes back to the 6th century B.C., while the oldest Indian fables in the Mahābhārata and in the Jātaka can only be traced back to the 4th century B.C. For Herodotos already knows Æsop as the poet of fables. But the bulk both of the 'Æsopian' and of the Indian fables go back to a time, when an intellectual interchange between Greece and India was already established, and when it was chronologically as possible that Indian fables should have come to Greece, as that Greek fables should have come to India. It is, therefore, not possible to decide the question of origin in general, but only in each individual case, and sometimes a decision is impossible. There can, for instance, be no doubt, that the fable of the ass in the lion's skin which is found in the Jātaka and in the *Pañcatantra* in India and in the Æsopian fables in Greece, can only have been invented once. But I can see no possibility of deciding with absolute certainty whether it was first invented in Greece or in India.

What India owes to Greece or Greece to India are much discussed problems in various departments of Indian literature.

Let us remember that in the 6th century B. C., the Persian Empire 'touched Greece at one extremity and India at the other.' (E. R. Bevan in the Cambridge History, 391 ff.) From the Persians the Greeks first learned the name Indoi, and from the Indians first heard the name Yona, Yavana or Ionians. Yavana was the name given to the people spread over part of the Balkan Peninsula, along the coast of Asia Minor and in the intermediate islands. Ever since Alexander's invasion in 326 B. C., there was a frequent intercourse between Greeks and Indians. And what is called 'Hellenism' and spread throughout the Roman Empire in the first centuries A. D. is Greek culture, steeped in Eastern elements. In this 'Hellenistic sea' as it has been called by a famous Greek scholar, East and West were inseparably united. And it is only natural that there should have been for centuries a mutual exchange of all kinds of tales, motives and ideas between Greece and India, and between India, Greece and Western Asia, and the original home of some of them will have to be looked for in India, of others further to the West. Just as the goods of the merchant, so also these stories were wandering to and fro. It was a mutual giving and taking.

We find, for instance, in the Jātaka the anecdote of a woman, whose husband, son and brother are to be executed, and who is granted by the king the life of one of them, the choice being left to herself. She chooses the life of the brother, for (she says) she could get another husband and another son, but never another brother. The same story is told by Herodotos of the wife of Tutaphernes and the same argumentation occurs in Sophokles' Antigone. In India, however, we find the same idea in the Rāmāyaṇa in connection with an old proverb, that everything in the world is easier to be got, than a full brother. The anecdote, therefore, is very old both in India and in Greece, and as there is nothing in it that is characteristically Greek or Indian, I see no possibility of deciding where it was first told.

Difficult to decide is also the question of the origin of the 'Judgment of Solomon.' In one of the Jātakas (Mahā-Ummagga-Jātaka, Nr. 546) we find quite a number of stories, in which the hero of the Jātaka, the boy Mahoṣadha gives proofs of his astounding cleverness by answering all kinds of difficult questions, solving puzzles and performing the most difficult tasks. The whole Jātaka has much in common with the tales of the wise Ahiqar (or Heykar), included in the Arabian Nights. Like King Solomon this wise boy Mahoṣadha decides the quarrel of two women about a child by testing their motherly love. He draws a line on the floor, places the child on it and tells the women to take hold of the child's hands and feet and try to pull him across the line: the woman who would be able to pull the child towards herself would be declared to be his mother. But as soon as they begin to pull, the child starts crying. At once one of the two women ceases to pull and is thus found out to be the real mother of the child. Most scholars are of opinion, that the Hebrew anecdote found in the I Book of Kings, is the original version, but some scholars have defended the originality of the Indian version, which is also known in China (where it forms the plot of a drama 'Hoei-lan-ki' or 'the circle of chalk'). It has also been suggested that there was an Egyptian book of wise judgments from which both the Hebrew and the Indian versions are derived. But it is difficult to say more than that the 'Judgment of Solomon' and similar anecdotes of wise judgments are widely spread in the literatures of the East and the West and that they seem to have a common origin.

But there are other cases where the Indian origin of stories can safely be asserted. Thus we find in the Jātaka book several versions of a story, in which a man along with some animals is saved from death by a passer-by. All the saved individuals promise their rescuer their help in case of need. But the saved man afterwards betrays the man who has saved his life, while all the animals prove their gratefulness to him by helpful acts. This story of the grateful beasts and the ungrateful man is far spread in world-literature. But only in India we find in Buddhist literature a whole set of such stories in all of which some animal—frequently an elephant—puts a man to shame by its kindness. About the Indian origin of all these stories there can be no doubt.

Again, in the Dhammapada commentary we find the famous story of Kisāgotamī, who in despair comes to the Buddha with her dead child in her arm, wanting him to bring her child again to life. The Buddha promises to do so, but on one condition: she must bring him a mustard seed from a house in which no human being has ever died. And poor Kisāgotamī wanders from house to house and everywhere she is told that either a father or a mother, a brother or a sister or a child has died, and at last she learns that death is the general lot of man, and comforted she enters the order of Buddhist nuns. Now a similar tale is found in the Greek, Arabic, Hebrew, Persian and Coptic versions of the legends of Alexander. But there cannot be the least doubt about the Indian origin of this legend. For the legend belongs to the class of consolation stories, of which we find many examples both in the Mahābhārata and in Buddhist and Jain literature.

Different from the question of the relation between Indian and Greek *fable* is the question, whether there has been any mutual influencing between Indian and Greek *novel*. The novel is a comparatively late production of Greek literature perhaps not older than Guṇāḍhya's *Bṛhatkathā*, though older than Daṇḍin, Subandhu and Bāṇa. There are, however, only few parallels between the Greek and the Indian novels. The details that have been compared seem to prove, that some Indian motives have found their way into Greek novels, but not that the Greek novel as a whole was borrowed from India.

I might mention here a strange coincidence occurring in Subandhu's novel 'Vāsavadattā.' Subandhu is very fond of hyperboles. Thus he describes the love pains of his heroine by saying: "The pain which this maiden has suffered......... could only be described, if the sky were a sheet of paper and the ocean an ink-pot, and if the scribe were God Brahman or the world-serpent Śeṣa the narrator, and then only in many thousands of world-periods." Now it is most interesting that the same hyperbole is found in the Talmud and in the Koran, where it is said, that God's greatness could only be described if the sky were a sheet of paper, etc. And strange enough, we find the same idea in a folk-song in many European countries which runs as follows:

> "And if the sky were made all of paper,
> And every star were a scribe,
> And every one of them were writing with a thousand hands,
> They could not fully describe my love."

One of the most disputed questions in the history of Indian literature is that regarding the supposed Greek influence on the Indian *Drama*. The theory that the Indian drama had been influenced by the *classical Greek comedy* has long been rejected. But in 1903 a book was published by Hermann Reich on the Greek *popular play*, the so-called *Mimos*, in which he traced its history throughout the whole literature of the world, and tried to prove, that strolling Greek actors also came to India. He pointed out a great many details, in which the popular Greek play agrees with such Indian dramas as the *Mṛcchakaṭika* and other Prakaraṇas. He has also shown that the Roman Mimus, which is an imitation of the Greek, has during the Middle Ages influenced the popular plays of Europe, especially of Italy. But Italian players came to the court of Queen Elizabeth to England, and have there greatly influenced the art of Shakespeare. And this explains again as Reich argues, the striking similarity between the Shakespearean and the Indian drama that has often been pointed out.

Now we know that the beginnings of the Indian drama have to be looked for in the ancient ballad poetry, mostly connected with religious worship. In so far the drama was certainly indigenous in India. But the poets who introduced the drama into literature, also imitated the popular performances of strolling players. And it is just *possible*, that among these strolling players there were also Greeks, who had come to India in the train of Bactrian and other foreign rulers in the North West of India. But I could not admit more than the *possibility* of such an influence—not on the origin—but on the development of the Indian drama. For it may be urged against the Greek influence, that the Indian drama as we know it, has an entirely national Indian character. If we look at a Gandhāra sculpture, the influence of Greek art strikes us at once. If we find in Indian astronomical or astrological works Greek technical terms, we cannot doubt, that Greek influence has been at work. There is no such thing in the drama. If there was any Greek influence on the Indian drama it can only have been a very superficial one.

I said that there was no doubt about the Greek influence in Indian astronomy and astrology. And I must say a few words about Indian and Greek science. It was indeed under the influence of *Greek astronomy,* that *Indian astronomy* which had existed long before, received its scientific character. The principal doctrines of the Sūryasiddhānta are those of Greek astronomy. In its introductory verses we are told that Sūrya revealed these doctrines to the Asura Maya in the city of *Romaka,* which means either Rome or Alexandria. What we learn from Varāhamihira in his *Pañcasiddhāntikā* about the contents of *Romaka Siddhānta* and the *Paulisa-Siddhānta* is distinctly Greek astronomy and the name of Paulisa is most probably, as Alberuni already suggested, Paulus of Alexandria.

That Indian *astrology* too, though it had existed long ago, developed under Greek influence, is proved by a verse found in the *Vṛddha-Garga-Saṃhitā,* one of the oldest works on astrology, where it is said: "Though the Greeks are barbarians, yet this science is well established among them; therefore even they are honoured like Ṛṣis, how much more a Brahman who devotes himself to astrology." Varāhamihira's *Bṛhajjātaka* which treats of horoscopy, is entirely influenced by Greek astrology. The Sanskrit terms *Jātaka* and *horā* are synonymous and *horā* is a Greek word.

*Mathematics* and *Geometry* are indigenous Indian sciences, and it is highly probable that the system of writing numerical figures now adopted in the whole civilised world was first invented in India. Geometry also, as we find it in the Sulbasūtras, is not influenced by the Greeks and the so-called 'Pythagorean theorem' was known to the authors of the Sulbasūtras.

In *medical* science we find many analogies between Indian and Greek theories, and some of these may have to be explained by Greek influence, though Indian medical science is certainly independent in its origin. Some medicaments such as opium and mercury, and in diagnostics the art of taking the *pulse*, have been borrowed from Persian and Arabic medicine. On the other hand, Indian medical works were translated into Arabic and Persian at an early time. Tibet, Ceylon and Farther India have entirely adopted Indian medicine.

Numerous are the points of agreement between *Indian and Greek philosophy*. But competent scholars differ very much as to the question of a historical connection between the two. Thus the similarity between the doctrines of the Eleatics (Xenophanes, Parmenides) and the Vedānta is obvious. But most scholars are more inclined to think that this similarity is due to a parallel development than to borrowing. Garbe, the greatest authority on Sāṃkhya Philosophy in Europe, has made it very probable, that Sāṃkhya Philosophy has been of influence on the philosophical ideas of Heraklitos, Empedokles, Anaxagoras, Demokritos and Epikuros. Keith denies any such influence. And it must be admitted that here too, parallel development is possible. On the other hand, it seems to me to be proved that Pythagoras was influenced by the Indian Sāṃkhya. Nor have I any doubt that the *Gnostic* and *Neo-Platonic* philosophies have been influenced by Indian philosophical ideas.

The late Mahāmahopādhyāya Satish Chandra Vidyābhushaṇa has tried to prove that Indian logic has developed under the influence of Aristotelian doctrines on the syllogism. Other scholars have suggested that the atomistic theory of the Vaiśeṣika system arose under the influence of the same theory as taught by the Greek philosopher Empedokles.

On all these questions the last word has not yet been said and will perhaps never be said.

Nor has the last word been said on the question what India may contribute to world-literature *in future*. Only fifty years ago very little was known in the West of ancient Buddhist literature,—to-day many of the Buddhist Pāli texts are read by a large and interested public in English and German translations.

Comparatively little of the great epics of India is known in the West outside the circle of scholars. It is not at all unlikely that much more of it will by future translations become part of world-literature.

And only within the last ten years the works of our own Poet Rabindranath Tagore have spread all over the civilised world by translations into Western and Eastern languages. His works are read and appreciated by old and young in the West and I can tell you from my own experience that you will hardly find a bookshop in Germany, Austria or Czechoslovakia where R. Tagore's books are not exhibited in the show windows.

If we read the signs of the times rightly, there is every probability that India will contribute as much to world-literature in the future as it has done in the past.

And let us hope that these contributions will help to strengthen the knowledge that *East and West have never been separate, and can never be separated.* Many a question I raised in this evening's lecture had to remain unanswered. But however desirable it may be for the historian to come to definite conclusions about all these problems and questions, it is only *one* lesson we learn from all the comparisons between Indian literature and the literatures of the world—the great lesson *not only of the unity of East and West, but of the unity of mankind.* Whether we have to explain the coincidences I pointed out between the literatures of the world by mutual borrowing and influencing, or whether we have to assume that the same ideas sprang up independently among different nations,—the conclusion must always be the same, that *the human mind is the same all over the world.* How else could it be possible, that Indian ideas, Indian tales, Indian poetry appealed and appeal to so many other nations, that foreign ideas could be infused into Indian literature, and that there was this constant mutual exchange of ideas between the peoples of the East and the West!

The Vedānta teaches that he only can be saved who *knows* the Unity. Civilised mankind also can only escape that ruin which is terribly near, by the *knowledge* that all *disunion* is infatuation, is Māyā, and that *union* only is real, is truth. May India help the West in realising this truth![1]

M. WINTERNITZ

[1] Lecture delivered at the Calcutta University, 18th September, 1923.

## KAUTILIYA ARTHASASTRA

### THE SCIENCE OF ECONOMICS AND POLITICS IN ANCIENT INDIA.

You all know the Indian doctrine of the *trivarga*, that is, of the three aims of life, *viz.*, *dharma*, *artha*, and *kāma*. According to this doctrine every man should strive to satisfy his spiritual needs by fulfilling his religious and moral duties (*dharma*), his material needs by acquiring the necessaries of life, property, wealth and power (*artha*), and his sexual desires by following the dictates of love (*kāma*). In later times *mokṣa* or salvation was added as a fourth and highest aim of life. The doctrine of the *trivarga* is at least as old as the grammarian Patañjali who is generally believed to have lived in the 2nd century B.C. It is often mentioned in the Māhābhārata and in the Manusmṛti. But it is not known since when there existed separate schools and śāstras for each of the three parts of the *trivarga* and more specially since when there existed a separate Arthaśāstra. For we know that the earliest Dharmaśāstras, the Dharmasūtras, are closely connected with the Vedāṅga literature, the Śrauta and Gṛhyasūtras, and may go back to the fifth century B. C. But though in the Caranavyūha, one of the Atharvaveda pariśiṣṭas, the Arthaśāstra is said to be an Upaveda of the Ṛgveda, it certainly has nothing to do with the Veda. This theory of Upavedas is only due to the desire of the Brahmans to connect all Śāstras, even the most profane of all, with their own domain, the Veda, and thus to make them Brāhmaṇical.

The very term *Arthaśāstra* shows that it has nothing to do with religious matters. It denotes all doctrines and books concerned with practical life, technics, economics, administration and politics. The most important branch of the Arthaśāstra is politics which as a separate science is also called *Nītiśāstra*. But since a knowledge of technical and economical matters is also required for the king and therefore forms part of 'politics,' the terms Arthaśāstra and Nītiśāstra are often used as synonyms. As in ancient India Government was as a rule monarchical, this science is also called *Rājanīti or Rājaśāstra* "the science of politics for kings"; and as the principal means of politics was force and punishment, it is also called *Daṇḍanīti, i.e.*, 'politics by means of punishment.'

In the Śāntiparva of the Mahābhārata, the gods and sages Bṛhaspati, Viśālākṣa, Uśanas, Mahendra Sahasrākṣa, Manu Prācetasa, Bhāradvāja and Gauraśiras are mentioned as Rājaśāstrapranetāraḥ, 'propounders of the science for kings.' Here as elsewhere the same teachers appear both as authors of Dharmaśāstras and of Arthaśāstras. It seems that the Arthaśāstra was originally taught in the schools of the Dharmaśāstra among the 'duties of the king' (rājadharmāḥ), but that at some time it branched off from the Dharmaśāstra and was taught in separate schools of Arthaśāstra. Even in the old Dharmaśāstras, *e.g.*, in the Apastambīya Dharmasūtra, some subjects of the Arthaśāstra, such as the building of towns and palaces, tolls and taxes and military matters are treated. But the metrical Dharmaśāstras already presuppose a separate Arthaśāstra.

Yājñavalkya and Nārada lay down the rule that in case of a conflict between Dharmaśāstra and Arthaśāstra the former has to be followed. There are also essential differences between the two Śāstras with regard to the way in which they treat of judicial procedure. What is important for the one, is of secondary importance for the other. Thus the Arthaśāstra recommends the use of torture in judicial proceedings and says nothing about ordeals, while the Dharmaśāstra only mentions the latter.

The chief difference, however, between the two Śāstras is one of principle. The Dharmaśāstra teaches *duties* which are supposed to rest on Śruti, or the revealed texts; it teaches what according to Brāhmaṇical law—according to the *Dharma*—ought to be done. On the other hand, the Arthaśāstra teaches the *methods* by which material success, *artha*, is to be obtained, whether these methods agree with religion and morality or not. *Nīti* is well defined by Māgha (Śiśupālavadha, II, 30)[1] as having only two aims: one's own rising and conquering the enemy. Therefore the Buddhists would never have anything to do with the Arthaśāstra and declared the Nīti as lying.

Nevertheless, as it is the custom in India, even for such a worldly science as the Arthaśāstra divine origin is claimed. We read in the Śāntiparvan of the Mahābhārata, that the creator Brahman himself had composed a great Sāstra in no less than 1,00,000 lessons (Adhyāyas) in which the whole *trivarga* was explained. For the benefit of the world and for the sake of establishing the *trivarga* he proclaimed the science of Daṇḍanīti. This Nītiśāstra, we are told, was first learnt by the large-eyed (Viśālākṣa) Śiva and was shortened by him to only 10,000 Adhyāyas in view of the shortness of man's life. This was further abbreviated by the god Indra to 5,000 Adhāyayas, by Bṛhaspati to 3,000, and finally by Uśanas to 1,000 Adhyāyas.

We see from this passage that Indian tradition ascribes the origin of the Arthaśāstra to Bṛhaspati, who is also known as a teacher of the Lokāyata or materialistic system of philosophy. And there is no doubt, that Lokāyata and Arthaśāstra are closely connected. A text of the Bārhaspatya Arthaśāstra has been published but this is certainly not the old Arthaśāstra of Bṛhaspati, as little as the work published as Śukranīti is the old Arthaśāstra of Śukra or Uśanas.

The oldest and the most important, I might almost say, the only real Arthaśāstra that has come down to us is the Kauṭilīya Arthaśāstra. This is one of the most remarkable

[1] आत्मोदयः परज्यानिर्द्वयं नीतिरितीयती ।

books in the whole of Sanskrit literature. There is, in fact, no other work that gives us so much rich information on the social, economical and political conditions in ancient India than this Arthaśāstra ascribed to Kauṭilya, the minister of the Maurya king Chandragupta. That such a work was in existence had been known to German scholars as long ago as 1874 and 1883, when *Th. Aufrecht* and *Th. Zachariae* first referred to it. But the text has only become known in 1909 by the edition of *R. Shama Sastri*, to whom we are also indebted for an English translation, published in 1915. A revised edition of the text was published by the same scholar in 1919.

The oldest form in which all scientific subjects were taught in the Brāhmaṇical schools, was the Sūtra style, a kind of aphoristic prose, in which chiefly nouns, especially abstract nouns and compounds and hardly any verbs were used. The purpose of these Sūtras was to say as much as possible in as few words as possible. You know the saying of Patañjali, that a Sūtrakāra rejoices over the saving of half a short vowel as much as over the birth of a son. These Sūtras had to be learnt by heart by the pupil, and could only be understood with the help of a commentary given by the teacher. When the Brāhmaṇical schools were replaced by special schools for each branch of science, the Sūtra style was retained, but generally the Sūtras were followed immediately by a Bhāṣya or commentary, composed by the author himself or one of his pupils. In this way a characteristic Bhāṣya style was developed, in which the disputations of the pundits in the Sabhās are reflected. The best example of this Bhāṣya style is the elegant prose of Patañjali's Mahābhāṣya. But even before there were any schools or Śāstras, doctrines both of *dharma* and of *artha* had been taught in the form of memorial verses (Kārikās) and maxims. Numerous such maxims, containing rules of conduct for the king, are found in many parts of the Mahābhārata. Now the Kauṭilīya

Arthaśāstra is composed in a mixture of Sūtra and Bhāṣya style, occasionally the prose is interrupted by memorial verses or maxims, mostly ślokas, but sometimes also verses in Upajāti metre. One or several verses are always found at the end of an Adhyāya.

So much about the style of the work. Now let me give you a very short account of its contents.

The first Adhikaraṇa treats according to its title of *Vinaya*, that is, of discipline or the education of princes. A prince should be instructed in philosophy (Ānvīkṣikī), in the Veda (Trayī), in economics (Vārtā), and in politics (Daṇḍanīti). Philosophy is the foundation of all other sciences, for it sharpens the mind and makes it fit for thinking, speaking and acting properly in all conditions of life both in adversity and in good luck. By reasoning (hetubhiranvīkṣamāṇā) philosophy helps to discern in the Veda what is right and wrong, in economics what is useful and what is useless, in politics what are right and what are false methods. Knowledge of Vedas and Vedāṅgas is necessary for the prince, in order to know the duties of the castes and stages of life (āśrama). For as regards the duties of men, the Arthaśāstra fully acknowledges the Brāhmaṇical doctrine of *Svadharma*, that is, of different laws and duties for each caste and āśrama. After the tonsure ceremony (caula) the prince should learn writing and arithmetic. After the Upanayana he should study philosophy and Veda under learned Brāhmaṇs (Śiṣṭebhyaḥ). Economics he should learn from the superintendents of the different departments and politics from theoretical and practical politicians. He should always keep intercourse with aged learned men, in order to make his education perfect. He should devote the morning to military training, the afternoon to hearing the Itihāsas, that is, to literary studies. But all education depends for its success on the controlling of one's senses (*indriyavijaya*). Therefore it is of the utmost importance that the prince should learn to control his organs of sense, and to conquer the group of six enemies (*Śatruṣaḍvarga*), *viz.*, lust, anger, greed, pride, haughtiness and vainglory.

But even the best ruler cannot hope for success, unless he has appropriate friends and servants. Hence several chapters are devoted to the choice of ministers and officials, and to the ways and means by which their character may be found out. For this purpose it is necessary to make use of all kinds of spies and to offer all sorts of temptations to them. Only thus their reliability can be ascertained.

This institution of spies is the subject of many chapters of the Arthaśāstra. The different kinds of spies and their methods are carefully described. There are spies in the disguise of disciples, of ascetics, of peasants, of merchants and female mendicants. Desperados (tīkṣṇa) and poisoners are ever ready to use violent means against traitors or enemies of the king. Cooks, barbers and other menials, persons in the disguise of hunchbacks, dwarfs, deaf or mute or blind people, nuns, singers, dancers, actors, prostitutes, etc., are especially fit for spying out the private life of ministers and courtiers. There are spies who are used only in one place, and wandering spies. And the spy service is carefully organised, the spies communicate with one another and with the head office by signs and secret writing. This organisation is used not only against enemies within and outside the state, but it is also spread over the whole country, in order to spy out citizens and country people as to their allegiance to the king. Loyal persons are rewarded, disaffected persons are got rid of rather by foul than by fair means. Spies are also employed for winning over adherents and for causing sedition in a neighbouring country of a hostile king. Ambassadors in foreign countries are also a kind of spies, and are always in communication with the headquarters of espionage organization.

A dreary chapter is that on *rājaputrarakṣaṇa*, in which the king is advised how to protect himself from his own sons, who are said to be a constant danger to him. 'From their very birth he should watch the princes, for princes are like crabs inclined to devour their begetters.'

The chapter on the daily duties of the king has been sarcastically quoted by the poet Daṇḍin in his Daśakumāra-carita. For according to the rules given here by Kauṭilya it would appear that there could not be any harder and more troublesome life than that of a ruler. Not one minute he is, according to these rules, left to himself, he has hardly time to sleep and he is in constant danger of his life. A whole chapter is devoted to the construction of the women's apartments in the royal palace, and the measures to be taken for the protection of the king in the seraglio. For nowhere is he in greater danger and many kings are known to have been assassinated in the women's apartments. And another chapter gives general rules as to how the life of the king is to be protected from danger of being poisoned or else assassinated.

The second Adhikaraṇa treats of the superintendents (adhyakṣa) of the different departments and of these departments themselves. Here we get the most detailed and most valuable information about such matters as the foundation of towns and villages, the distribution of land, the building of forts, financial administration, state revenue, the composition of royal writs, on gems, on mining, on industrial establishments, trade and commerce, forestry, armoury, weights and measures, on agriculture, on the supervision of the liquor trade, on shipping, on the regulation of prostitution, on cattle breeding, on horses and elephants, collection of taxes, on water works, markets, passports, etc. In the first chapter are included very interesting rules about the king's duty to provide for orphans, for the aged and the sick, for helpless women with child and for their new-born children. Here we also learn something about the corruption of officials in the financial department. They are never to be trusted, for—

"As it is not possible if you have honey or poison on your tongue, not to taste it, so it is for a king's official in the finance department impossible not to taste at least something of the 'king's money.' As with fish moving in water, it is impossible to know when they are drinking water so it is impossible with government officials to know when they take money for themselves."

In the chapter on the duties of the Nāgaraka or city superintendent we read of regulations for strangers coming into the town, of sanitary measures, and the duties of householders with regard to preventing danger from fire and helping when a fire has broken out.

The third Adhikaraṇa treats of civil law and shows much similarity with the law books of Yājñavalkya and Nārada. The fourth Adhikaraṇa is devoted to the *Kaṇṭaka-śodhana*, that is, the 'clearing of the land of thorns,' that is, of dangerous elements by police regulations and criminal law. Such thorns are all kinds of artizans who cheat their customers, careless physicians, dishonest merchants, musicians, dancers and similar folk. Such thieves who are not called thieves he should prevent from being a plague to the country.

To get rid of them, spies are largely employed. Some chapters treat on examination in case of sudden death, or trial by torture, and on different kinds of punishment.

The fifth Adhikaraṇa teaches all kinds of cunning and sometimes abominable methods which a king is advised to employ, in order to get rid of unreliable ministers, traitors and state enemies, who are too powerful to be dealt with openly. For instance, a spy is sent out to instigate the brother of a minister, suspected of high treason, and to take him to the king in audience. The king by promising to confer upon him the property of his brother, causes him to take the latter's life. And when he has murdered his brother by weapon or poison, he is put to death as a fratricide. Or, the king may send such a minister on an expedition for putting down some rebellious wild tribe or for some similar purpose. In an affray that ensues desperado-spies in the disguise of robbers who have been sent with the expedition army, shall murder the minister and it should be reported that he was killed in the battle. Or the king when going out to some war or hunting expedition, receives these ministers in audience. While they are with the king, desperado-spies with concealed weapons according to a previous arrangement, try to enter the audience hall, let themselves be caught and searched by the door-keepers and declare themselves to be accomplices of the minister. This is made known to the public, the ministers are put to death, and instead of the desperado-spies some other people are to be executed (anye vadhyāḥ).

In the second chapter of the same Adhikaraṇa the king is taught how to fill his empty treasury by all kinds of fair and foul means. First of all, if the regular taxes do not bring sufficient revenues, he should exact from peasants, merchants and tradesmen as much of taxes and dues as possible by threats and promises. Secret agents may also instigate rich people to voluntary gifts for which they are rewarded by honorary posts or by an umbrella, a turban, or an ornament. But also the property of religious communities and of temples as far as they are not assigned for the use of learned Brahmans (śrotriya), may, under some pretext or other, be appropriated to the king's treasury. The superintendent of temples and idols (devatādhyakṣa) may also collect a treasure from the different public shrines in forts and in the country and bring them to the king's treasury. Or, the king may have a shrine with an idol erected during the night and the news spread abroad that it had sprung up by itself and from the pilgrimages and processions he may derive profit. Or, spies disguised as saints (siddhasa), may cause a panic by announcing that there was a

Rākṣasa at a certain tree, and make the people bring gold to appease the demon.

Quite a number of devices are taught by which the king can not only replenish his treasury, but also at the same time, rid himself of his adversaries. For instance a quarrel is raised between the members of a suspected family, poisoners are engaged to poison one of them, the others are accused of the offence, and their property is confiscated.

Very interesting is the third chapter of this Adhikaraṇa, which contains a complete list of the salaries and wages of all Government officials and king's servants from the highest priests and ministers with an annual salary of 48,000 paṇa down to the menial servants who receive only 60 paṇas a year.

But the Arthaśāstra contains not only instructions for the king, but also, in the two last chapters of this Adhikaraṇa, teaches ministers and courtiers how to gain and retain the king's favour and also how to get all power into their own hands.

The VI th and VII th Adhikaraṇas treat of politics in the narrower sense of the word. Here we find the same method of classification and definition as in other śāstras. We have here the seven Prakṛtis or elements of the kingdom (king, minister, country, fort, treasury, army and friend); the maṇḍalas of friendly and hostile neighbours with their divisions and sub-divisions and again the six methods of politics, peace, war, neutrality, mobilisation, alliance and double policy (dvaidhībhāva). These two Adhikaraṇas contain the most detailed instructions on the methods of foreign policy.

The VIIIth Adhikaraṇa treats of the Vyāsanas or evils of an empire, that is, on the one hand the vices of the rulers (hunting, gambling, drinking and women) and on the other hand of calamities, such as epidemics, floods, fire, etc.

The following Adhikaraṇas, IX and X are entirely devoted to military matters, the recruiting and organisation of armies, etc. At the beginning of a battle the king is told how to stimulate the soldiers by speeches, supported by priests and astrologers who describe the joys of heaven awaiting the brave warrior, and the tortures of hell destined for the cowards. But as it is not always possible to conquer the enemy by force, cunning also must be employed. For, as it is said in a verse:

"The arrow shot by the archer,
May kill one or even none,
But cunning employed by the wise,
Will kill even the child in the womb."

This verse leads over to the following Adhikaraṇas (XI, XII) in which all kinds of sinister methods are taught, by which an enemy may be conquered. Spies, desperados, poisoners, and prostitutes may be freely employed. Warrior chiefs who get their livelihood by warfare such as those of Kāmbhoja, Surāṣṭra, or the Licchivikas, Vṛjikas, Mallakas, etc.—may be either won as allies or separated by creating disunion among them. For the latter purport courtezans, as female spies, are specially recommended. The employment of wicked women and the abuse of religious institutions are most conspicuous in the methods recommended to a weak king for conquering a stronger one.

Thus, a king may send spies into the hostile country not only in order to spy out everything, but also through spies in the disguise of meat or liquor dealers, to poison the people. Or, in places of worship in the enemy's country where people gather for pilgrimage and sacrifices, he may secretly have machines erected, by which walls or rocks will fall down and kill numbers of enemies.

It is strange that the same Kauṭilya who in many places of the Arthaśāstra proves himself to be an orthodox follower of Brāhmaṇism and often recommends the performance of religious rites, and always admonishes the king to protect Brahmans and ascetics and to take due regard of their privileges,—that the same Kauṭilya has no scruples whatever in recommending stratagems which can only be called an abuse of religious institutions, and a speculation on the credulousness and religiosity (or you may call it superstitiousness, for what is superstition to the one is religion to the other) of the people.

Thus, if the king wishes to seize hold of a village in the enemy's country, he should encourage his own people and cause panic among the enemies by having accounts spread abroad of his being omniscient and in direct communication with deities. Whenever he has got some information about the enemy's country through his spies, or through letter-carrying pigeons, he has the news of his knowledge and rumours about his knowing everything through superhuman agency spread abroad. This fame of having intercourse with divine beings may be acquired in the following ways, for instance:

The king, when worshipping at the fire-altar or at a shrine, should hold conversations with the god of fire or the deity of the shrine, while in reality spies are, by means of a subterraneous passage, hidden in the fire-altar or in the interior of the hollow statue of the god and speak out of them. In the same way he may be found to hold converse with Nāgas, who are in reality, spies rising up from the water. He may also make use of such magical tricks as are generally performed by jugglers at night, in order to appear on the surface of the water talking with god Varuṇa or with Nāga maidens. Astrologers and Paurāṇikas or rather spies disguised as such should also contribute to spread the fame of the king's supernatural powers and tell stories of his having received weapons and treasures from heavenly beings, or of his understanding the language of beasts and birds.

In order to get a hostile king into his power stratagems like the following are recommended to a conqueror:

A spy in the guise of an ascetic with shaved head or braided hair and followed by a great number of disciples with braided hair (who of course are also spies), should take up his abode near the capital city of the enemy, living in the cave of a mountain. Bringing presents of roots and fruits the disciples should go to the palace and invite the king and the ministers to see the venerable ascetic. When the king arrives at the spot, the ascetic shall tell him stories about ancient kings and countries and then he shall say: "Every time when I get a hundred years old, I enter into the fire and come out young again. Now here in your presence I will enter the fire for the fourth time; it was necessary for me to have you brought here; choose three boons." When the king agrees the ascetic should say: "You must live here for seven (days and) nights with wife and children before the performance of the miracle." And while the king is staying there, a sudden attack shall be made on him.

While the unfair methods of conquest are described at great length, only one chapter is devoted to the 'honest' siege of a fortress. A very interesting chapter treats of the pacification of a conquered country. Here we read: "After having acquired a new territory the victorious king should cover the enemy's vices with his own virtues and shine out the enemy's virtues by doubling his own virtues. By strict observance of his duties, by bestowing rewards, privileges and honours, he should do everything that is pleasing and contributing to the welfare of the subjects......He should adopt the manners, costume, language and style of life of the people. And he shall follow their faith (bhakti) as regards local deities, processions, festivals and amusements......He should grant a general amnesty (sarvabandhanamokṣaṇam) and afford help to the distressed, the helpless, and the sick......On the Cāturmāsya festivals he should forbid the killing of animals for half a month, on the full moon nights for four days and on the (auspicious) Nakṣatra (day) of the king or the country for one day.

In this whole chapter the Arthaśāstra does not relinquish its *artha* point of view. For it recommends humanity, justice, benevolence and regard for the people's religious feelings not for the sake of dharma, but only as the best means by which a conquered country can be pacified and kept in possession.

The XIV Adhikaraṇa, called aupaniṣadikam is a treatise on witchcraft, difficult to understand. We find here recipes for the preparation of powders and mixtures for causing instantaneous death, blindness, madness, leprosy or other diseases and again others that enable a man to fast for a month or to change his colour or to make himself invisible or to walk on fire and the like.

The last Adhikaraṇa describes the plan of the whole work and gives a list of the logical methods employed. This list contains 32 items while the Pūrva Mîmāṃsā and the philosophical Bhāṣyas know only of five or six such methods.

From this short survey of the Kauṭilīya-Arthaśāstra it will be seen that it is a perfectly unique work that throws more light on life in ancient India than any other work of Indian literature. And it would be a precious work, even if it were not older than the seventh century A.D. when we find it actually quoted by Daṇḍin. But it would be perfectly invaluable if it really were as it pretends to be, the work of the minister of Maurya Candragupta and would thus belong to the 4th century B.C. It would then be the first and only dated literary document of Indian culture from such an early time. And nothing would be more desirable than to possess such a book. But for this very reason we must be careful, not to let our judgment be influenced by our desires, when examining the reasons which speak for and against assigning the work to Candragupta's minister.

Now on what ground is the work ascribed to Kauṭilya? There are, first of all, the statements found in the book itself. At the end of the first chapter which contains the table of contents we read

सुखग्रहणविज्ञेयं तत्त्वार्थपदनिश्चितम् ।
कौटिल्येन कृतं शास्त्रं विमुक्तग्रन्थविस्तरम् ॥

"This text book (*śāstra*) that is easy to grasp and to understand, in which the words and their meanings are accurately (tattvena) settled, has been composed by Kauṭilya, avoiding prolixity of the text."

At the end of the 10th chapter of the 2nd Adhikaraṇa, which treats of the execution of royal writs, we read

सर्व्वशास्त्राण्यनुक्रम्य प्रयोगमुपलभ्य च ।
कौटिल्येन नरेन्द्रार्थे शासनस्य विधिःकृतः ॥

"Having gone over all sciences (śāstrāṇi) and relying on practice, Kauṭilya has, for the sake of kings, composed the rules about writs."

At the end of the last chapter of the book we have the śloka

येन शास्त्रं च शस्त्रं च नन्दराजगता च भूः ।
अमर्षेणोद्धृतान्याशु तेन शास्त्रमिदं कृतं ॥

"This text-book has been composed by him, who quickly and impatiently raised the Arthaśāstra (from former imperfect text-books) passed his sword and took the earth that had passed to the Nandas (out of their hands)."

Finally, after the colophon, at the end of the whole book we find the verse (in bad metre):

दृष्ट्वा विप्रतिपत्तिं बहुधा शास्त्रेषु भाष्यकाराणाम् ।
स्वयमेव विष्णुगुप्तश्चकार सूत्रं च भाष्यं च ॥

"Seeing the manifold discrepancies in the text-books of the commentators, Viṣṇugupta himself composed both the Sūtra and the commentary."

Moreover, in many chapters we find discussions of different opinions, which regularly end by stating the opinion of the author with the words: इति कौटिल्यः "So says Kauṭilya."

What do all these statements prove? In my opinion, nothing more than that the work pretends to be composed by

Kauṭilya, just as the Mahābhārata in its introductory and concluding Adhyāyas pretends to be composed by Vyāsa, the Manu-Smṛti by Manu, or the Viṣṇu-Smṛti by the god Viṣṇu. And as regards the verse in which Kauṭilya says that he has taken the kingdom from the Nandas, it seems to me to be very improbable, that the real minister in a book, written by the order or intended for his king, would have written such words which could not be very pleasing to the king. Or, if we assume that he wrote the book after Candragupta's death, the latter's successor would certainly have resented such a statement. *Prof. Jacobi*, it is true, sees in this verse the proud self-consciousness of a great statesman, of the "Indian Bismarck," as he calls Kauṭilya. But I doubt, whether the contents of the Arthaśāstra justify the assumption that it is the work of a statesman and not of a Pundit. For we find in it exactly the same predilection for endless and pedantic classifications and definitions as in other scientific works composed by Pundits. For instance, the sovereign, the minister, the territory with its subjects, the fort, the treasury, the army, and the ally form the *seven* prakṛtis or constituents of a kingdom (or State), and we have a long list of the good qualities which each of them should have. Or what has been called the 'inter-state relations,' is a kind of Geometry of the situation of the States. The Vijigīṣu (who, of course, is always a model of virtue, possessed of the best Prakṛtis, and is the embodiment of statesmanship) with his neighbouring kings forms a Maṇḍala or 'Circle of States,' consisting of 12 states, in which the immediate neighbour is always the enemy, the neighbour of the enemy always the ally. This method of classifying is well known to us from other śāstras and certainly looks more like the work of Pundits than of a statesman.

We also find lengthy discussions after the manner of the śāstras as for instance on the choice of ministers. Shall a king choose his playmates as ministers? No, they would have no respect for him. Shall he choose those who share their secrets with him? No, for they also know his secrets, and will make him dependent on them. Shall he choose those who have saved him from some danger? No, for this only proves their faithfulness, not their cleverness. Shall he choose those whose fathers and grandfathers were already ministers of the royal family? No, for they would have too much power over the king and try to rule themselves. Shall he appoint new ministers who are versed in the Nītiśāstra? No, it is not enough to know the Śāstras, a minister should also understand business. He should appoint as ministers such men, who are distinguished by good family, cleverness, honesty, braveness and faithfulness.

But we also find mere quibbling on such questions as: which is the worst of the four voices: hunting, gambling, addiction to women and drinking? Or, what is worse, quarrels among the people, or quarrels among kings? and so on.

And the numerous discussions, in which the opinions of different teachers (such as Bhāradvāja, Viśālākṣa, Parāśara, etc.) or of different schools (Mānavas, Bārhaspatyas, Auśanasas) are quoted, as opposed to that of Kauṭilya, can only be explained by assuming that the Nītiśāstra was taught in schools long before the composition of our Arthaśāstra. These discussions generally end by stating the author's opinion with the words: iti Kauṭilyaḥ. It is, of course, possible that an author may state his opinion in this way. But we generally find this mention of the name of a teacher in texts emanating from schools. Thus, Jaimini is mentioned in the Pūrvamīmāṁsāsūtra, Bādarāyaṇa in the Vedāntasūtra, Baudhāyana in the Baudhāyana Dharmaśāstra, but I do not think that Patañjali in the Mahābhāṣya ever states his opinion by saying: iti Patañjaliḥ.

The very name Kauṭilya which is given to the author of our work—he is never called Cāṇakya, and only once Viṣṇugupta in the final śloka which has all the appearance of a copyist's addition, for it follows after the last colophon—raises grave doubts as to his being the real author of the work. Kauṭilya means 'crookedness,' 'falsehood'; is it likely that Candragupta's minister should have called himself 'Mr. Crooked' or 'Crookedness personified'? I doubt it.

And what do we really know of Kauṭilya or Cāṇakya or Viṣṇugupta, as the minister of Candragupta is called? The Purāṇas unanimously report (in form of prophecy) that Kauṭilya destroyed the royal dynasty of the Nandas, and anointed the Maurya Candragupta king. They never mention a single name about his having been a teacher or an author. Patañjali in his Mahābhāṣya mentions the Mauryas and the Sabhā of Candragupta, but says nothing about his famous minister. Whatever else is reported about Cāṇakya or Kauṭilya, belongs to the realm of legend and poetry, thus the story underlying the drama Mudrārākṣasa, and the stories found in Somadeva's Kathāsaritsāgara and in Hemachandra's Pariśiṣṭaparvan. In these stories Cāṇakya, as he is generally called, appears as a type of the clever and unscrupulous diplomatist, but never as a writer or teacher. Only in the first act of the Mudrārākṣasa Cāṇakya is accompanied by his disciple.

In or about 322 B.C. Candragupta came to the throne. In 302 B.C. the Greek Megasthenes came as the ambassador of Seleukos Nikator to Candragupta's court and stayed there for many years. Of his account of India—The Indika,—which has formed the basis of all later reports on India in the writings of Greek and Roman authors, only fragments have been preserved. It is strange enough that neither Megasthenes nor any other Greek or Roman author knows anything about the minister of King Candragupta.

Radhakumud Mookerji, Narendranath Law, Vincent Smith and Dr. Thomas have pointed out some agreements between the account of Megasthenes and the condition described in the Kauṭilīya-Arthaśāstra, from which they concluded that the author of the latter and the Greek Megasthenes must have been contemporaries. But a closer examination and comparison of the two accounts as it has been made by my pupil Dr. Otto Stein, has shown that Megasthenes agrees with the Kauṭilya as a rule only in such things as would not change at different periods of time, for instance, irrigation by means of canals, choice of sites for fortresses, the methods of taming and training elephants, the custom of polygamy, the longing for children, the employment of spies, etc. On the other hand Megasthenes differs widely from Kauṭilya in the most essential details. Thus Megasthenes speaks of mile stones [1] on the roads, which are unknown to Kauṭilya. According to Megasthenes water for irrigation is carefully distributed to private people, while Kauṭilya knows nothing of such a distribution of water, but mentions private water works. Megasthenes speaks of wooden ramparts for fortresses, as also the excavations at Pāṭaliputra (Patna) have shown remnants of wooden structures of the Maurya time. Kauṭilya, however, says that the ramparts should be made of stones, and emphatically adds, that they should not be made of wood on account of danger from fire. According to Megasthenes no private person was allowed to possess elephants or horses, but they were the monopoly of the king. Kauṭilya knows nothing of such a monopoly. In Mṛcchakaṭika also Vasantasenā owns elephants. What Megasthenes reports about metals, mining, metallurgy points to a more primitive time than the numerous details given by Kauṭilya about these things which show a great advance in technical knowledge and in Chemistry.

It is of great importance, that Kauṭilya among the different kinds of gold mentions artificial gold, made from other metals by chemical process in which mercury is used. Now the use of mercury both in alchemy and in medicine is well known in India, but is found only in later literature. Even P. C. Ray, in his excellent history of Indian Chemistry,

[1] Sign-boards noting turnings, and distances put up at intervals 'ten stades.'

who believes that alchemy is indigenous in India, cannot trace it back any further than the earliest Tantric text in the 5th or the 6th century A.D. In medical works mercury is mentioned only once in Caraka's treatise, once in the Bower MS. (4th century A.D.) and twice in the Suśruta. It is entirely unknown in earlier literature. And I am inclined to think that this chapter on minerals is a strong proof of later origin of the Arthaśāstra.

To return to Megasthenes, he tells us that women follow the king, when he is going out to hunt, that armed women accompany him on war chariots or horses or elephants both on his hunting expeditions and into battle, and he adds that anybody approaching the women is killed. Kauṭilya knows only of men who accompany the king when going out hunting.

Megasthenes emphatically states that there is no slavery in India. Both the Arthaśāstra and the Dharmaśāstras know different kinds of male and female slaves.

Megasthenes says, that the agriculturists who are the majority of the population never take part in war or in other public services but their land is never devastated in war. Kauṭilya, however, mentions separate armies consisting of Brāhmans, of Kṣatriyas, Vaiśyas and Śūdras amongst whom were no doubt also agriculturists. From Kauṭilya we also know that war in ancient India was as much a plague for the tillers of the soil as it is now in all countries.

In one passage (Kaut., pp. 331 f.) the question is discussed, whether one's own army or that of the enemy is a greater plague for the people, and Kauṭilya decides that "the enemy's army is a plague for the whole country, for it oppresses by robbing, burning, destroying, and abducting." Kauṭilya also says (p. 404) that before proceeding with a siege the king must begin to damage the neighbouring country by the destruction of agricultural produce, of standing crops, of their trade, and by causing the people to run away.

But the greatest difference between Kauṭilya and Megasthenes is found in their respective accounts of the administration. More especially the organization of the financial bureaucracy as described by Megasthenes is quite different from that found in the Arthaśāstra. As to the local or municipal administration Megasthenes gives a great many details about six corporations each consisting of five officials, while Kauṭilya knows nothing about such corporations but only of individual officials who have different agenda.

The military organization also as described by Megasthenes, is essentially different from that which Kauṭilya has in view. According to Megasthenes the Indians had a *navy* with a commander or admiral (υαναρχοζ) who has five officials under him. There is not the slightest hint in the Arthaśāstra that a fleet for military purposes existed at all. Kauṭilya only knows of a Nāvadhyakṣa, a superintendent of ships, who has entirely to deal with fiscal and commercial matters. Megasthenes again speaks of six bodies of five military officials each, one for the navy, one for the bullock-teams, one for the infantry, one for the horse, one for the chariots, and one for the elephants. Kauṭilya knows nothing about the use of bullock teams for military purposes, nor of the six pentads of military officials.

In some cases the descriptions of Megasthenes may be inaccurate or coloured for tendencious purposes, but in other cases he evidently describes social and political conditions which are different from those existing in the time when the Kauṭilīya Arthaśāstra was written. At any rate it can no longer be asserted that Kauṭilya and Megasthenes are in full agreement and therefore must be contemporaries.

If we look at the contents of the work itself, we find that it treats not only of politics, but of a great many subjects of administration which requires the knowledge of specialists in architecture, in agriculture, in mining, mineralogy, and chemistry, in military matters, etc. It is quite impossible that one man should have been a specialist in all these branches of knowledge. It might be said, and it has been suggested by *Jacobi*, that Kauṭilya had officials of different departments as collaborators. This is possible. But it seems to me to be more probable that there existed special treatises on all these topics, which the author of the Arthaśāstra included in his work with little alterations, just as he made ample use of previous works on politics in the narrower sense of the word. Therefore our work begins with the words :

पृथिव्या लाभे पालने च यावन्त्यर्थशास्त्राणि पूर्व्वाचार्य्यैः
प्रस्थापितानि प्रायशस्तानि संहृत्यैकमिदमर्थशास्त्रं कृतम् ।

that is, "Extracting and summarizing almost all the Arthaśāstras which have been propounded by previous teachers with a view of winning and maintaining the earth, this one Arthaśāstra has been composed."

That such special treatises were incorporated in the Arthaśāstra, is also made probable by the fact that sometimes the same subject is treated in different chapters. But this presupposes that at the time of the composition of the Arthaśāstra there existed a rich literature not only on politics, but also on economics and all kinds of technical arts. There even existed works on the diseases of trees (Gulma vṛkṣāyurveda). It is at least not very probable that such a highly developed technical literature existed in or before the 4th century B. C.

What literature, besides this Arthaśāstra literature, was known at the time of the composition of the Kauṭilīya may be seen from the first chapters on the education of princes. The Veda and the Vedāṅgas were known, as well as an epic narrative and didactic literature. The king should devote the afternoon to the hearing of Itihāsas (Itihāsa śravaṇe). And itihāsa is here (p. 10) defined as including Purāṇa (legendary and mythological lore), itivṛttam (history), ākhyāyikā (tales and stories), udāharaṇam (examples, fables), dharmaśāstra and Arthaśāstra. The latter cannot mean manuals of law and politics, but only didactic poetry (maxims, dialogues and fables) in which *dharma* and artha were taught. Of philosophical literature there seem to have existed works on Sāṃkhya, Yoga, and Lokāyata. For *ānvīkṣikī* (vidyā) the 'science of investigating' is defined as including these three systems. But it is difficult to think, that no other philosophical systems existed. Probably Vedānta and perhaps also Pūrvamīmāṃsā were included in the term *trayī*, 'theology.' Certainly the way of arguing by stating first the *pūrvapakṣa*, the most obvious opinion which, however, is not adopted and then the *uttarapakṣa* the opinion adopted by Kauṭilya shows an acquaintance with the Pūrvamīmāṃsā. And the last chapter of the whole work, in which 32 methodical artifices are enumerated which have been used by the author shows an acquaintance with a fully developed canon of logic. Of the Lokāyata literature nothing has come down to us. It is not impossible that what was later developed in Nyāya and Vaiśeṣika schools, was originally taught in the Lokāyata. At any rate, it is difficult to believe that the author of our work was not acquainted with any other systems of philosophy but the Sāṃkhya, Yoga and Lokāyata.

Besides the stories of the Mahābhārata and Rāmāyaṇa, many legends are alluded to the sources of which are unknown. But they are all Brāhmaṇical legends. And the whole Arthaśāstra shows, that its author was a strict adherent of Brāhmanism, and that he presupposes a social system entirely founded on Brāhmaṇic religion and custom. In performing his duties the king is always surrounded by priests. The sacrificial priest (Ṛtvij), the teacher (ācārya) and the Purohita receive the same highest salary (48,000 paṇas) as the prime minister, the Commander of the army, the heir-apparent (yuvarāja), the queen dowager and the first queen. (By receiving such a high salary, the author adds, they will not be discontented and not yield to temptation.)

Absolutely Brāhmaṇical is the teaching of the Svadharma, that is of a different law for each of the four castes and the four Āśramas (stages of life). In the chapter on *ind iyavijaya* we find as examples of wicked kings who did not control their senses, in the first line, kings who offended the Brāhmaṇs. Great importance is attached to the performance of religious ceromonies. In contradiction to other teachers, Kauṭilya says, that the best way to protect a king from his own sons is to perform the prescribed sacrifices and other religious rites after conception in order that a good son may be born, and after birth, that he may grow up without becoming a danger to his father.

In the daily life of the king, his performing the religious rites is most essential. In the morning be receives the benedictions of the priests (Ṛtvij, ācārya, purohita) and before going to the darbar, he must circumambulate a cow with its calf and a bull. He shall personally attend to the cases concerning gods, heritical sects, learned Brāhmiṇs, cows, sacred places, ascetics and Yogins. Priests and learned Brāhmiṇs, should be endowed with land. Forests for Veda study and Som growing (ब्रह्मसोमारण्यानि) shall be given to Brāhmiṇs and groves for performing austerities to ascetics. Worship of fire (*agnipūja*) is recommended as a protection against danger from fire, worship of rivers (*nadīpūja*) as a protection against flood, mountains are worshipped to avert danger from tigers. During droughts Indra, Gangā, Parvata and Mahakaccha are to be worshipped. Against epidemics Śānti and Prāyaścitta rites are performed by Siddhas and Tāpasas. Against cattle diseases nirājana (waving of lights in cowsheds) and worship of svadaivata is helpful. Rats may be destroyed (by keeping cats, mungoose and by witch-craft rites), but on full moon days rats are worshipped, and there is also a fine for killing rats that have been caught. It is similar with snakes.

A fine of 100 paṇas is prescribed for a Caṇḍāla who touches an Ārya woman and the same fine for one who entertains at rites for gods or ancestors Buddhists (Śakyas) Ajivikas and other ascetics of Śūdra origin (śūdrapravrajit).

There is a strange discrepancy between this strict Brāhmaṇical religiosity of our author, and the unscrupulousness with which the same author recommends all kinds of cunning tricks, in which religious rites and religiosity of the people are abused for political purposes of which I have given you some examples.

In this respect the author of the Kauṭiliya Arthaśāstra may be compared to *Macchiavelli* who does not shrink back from recommending the most abominable means for attaining an end, but is, at the same time, a most orthodox Christian and very religious. On the other hand, the often heard designation of Kauṭilya as 'the Indian *Macchiavelli*' is only partly justified. There is one marked difference between the Indian and the Italian author. The latter is above all a historian who derives his methods from the lesson of history. This historical point of view is entirely foreign to the author of the Arthaśāstra, who is a pure theoretician and only asks: which methods are useful to a monarch for gain and maintaining power and which are not? Both Macchiavelli and Kauṭilya, however, agree in standing 'jenseits von gut und bote,' that is in disregarding—for the time being—moral principles.

Some scholars, it is true, have tried to make out that Kauṭilya is a teacher of political morals. Benimadhab Barua in his 'History of Pre-Buddhistic Indian Philosophy' devotes a whole chapter to the Arthaśāstra under the heading of 'Political morals.' And Kalidas Nag in his very valuable thesis, recently published on Deplomatic theories in ancient India, repudiates the comparison of Kauṭilya with Machiavelli. He even speaks of Kauṭilya as having discussed the fundamental principles of international law. But I am afraid, we shall look in vain for anything that can be called 'law' at all in the inter-state relations with which Kauṭilya deals. It was Adam Smith, I believe, who first said (what has often been repeated since) that no human society can exist without any regulations of conduct being observed, and that even robbers, when they join in a gang, obey certain rules in their relations to one another. Thus in inter-state relations also, treaties are made which are kept as long as none of the parties is strong enough to break them. Kauṭilya gives detailed instructions not only about making but also about breaking treaties and setting hostages free. Even in the times of the Mahābhārata war there were rules about fair and unfair fighting. It was, for instance, considered unfair in a club fight, to strike against the thighs of the adversary—which did not however prevent the great hero, Bhīma from breaking Duryodhana's thighs with his club.

What Kauṭilya has to say about peace treaties and alliances has hardly anything to do with 'international law,' but is only part of the war-relations. Where war is impossible or not advisable some kind of treaty or alliance is made—until a king is strong enough to go to war.

Kalidas Nag even tries to make Kauṭilya a pacifist because in one passage he says: When the advantages of peace and war are alike, a king should conclude peace, as there is always loss and risk in war. But this rule is only the introduction to a chapter in which the principle is explained in detail which is stated in the previous chapter as a general rule. 'He who is *weaker* than the other shall make *peace*, he who is *stronger* shall wage *war*," (parasmād dhīyamanah samdadhīta, abhyucciyamāno vigṛhuīyāt).

Now it must be admitted that Kauṭilya, in the chapter on the education of princes and the duties of kings, lays great stress on restraint of senses (indriyavijaya), and on the king setting a good example to his subjects and having their welfare at heart. We have also seen that Kauṭilya strictly holds to the Brāhmaṇical laws of svadharma. But all this only means that he acknowledges morality (dharma) but not that he wants it to be applied in politics. It is also always tacitly assumed that the vijigīṣu 'he who wants to conquer' is the righteous king.

You know that in our days also the conqueror or the victorious party in war is always the righteous. And just as Kauṭilya occasionally pays his respects to morality, you will find in all proclamations of the great political leaders of our days that the most abominable things are alwys done in the name of justice, humanity and civilisation.

But let us return now to the question of the date and authorship of the work. From what I have said it will be clear that I cannot believe, that we have in the arthaśāstra really the work of the minister of the Maurya Chandragupta of the 4th century B.C. before us. This is also unlikely because Chandragupta was the ruler of a great Empire while the political doctrines of the Kauṭiliya Arthaśāstra only refers to a number of small states. In my opinion the work has been ascribed to him only, because the legendary Cāṇakya or Kauṭilya was the best known type of the cunning and unscrupulous minister who occurs so frequently both in the dramatic and narrative literature. For the same reason we find so many collections of Nīti maxims, which are ascribed to Cāṇakya and known as Cāṇakyanīti, Cāṇakyarājanīti, Cāṇakyaśataka and similar titles.

Yet I do not mean to say, that the Kauṭiliya Arthaśāstra is a modern work. It was certainly known to the author of the Tantrākhyāikā, the oldest version of the Pancatantra, which was probably composed sometime between 300 and 500 A.D. It was known to Vātsyāyana Pakṣilasvāmin, the author of the Nyāyabhāsya, it was the model after which Vatsyāyana Mallanāga formed his Kāmasūtra, and Daṇḍin in his Daśakumāracarita shows great familiarity with the book. The author of the Nyāyabhāṣya probably wrote about 350 or 400 A.D. Haranchandra Chakladar has tried to prove that the Kāmasūtra was composed between 225 A.D. and the beginning of the 4th century. I am rather inclined to place it in the 4th century. The Arthaśāstra may be a century or half a century older, and thus belongs to the 3rd century A.D. It is worth mentioning that Kauṭilya is not referred to even in the latest parts of the Mahābhārata where only Bṛhaspati and Śukra appear as Nīti teachers

But though it may be a disappointment, that we do not possess in the Arthaśāstra the original work of Chandragupta's famous minister of the 4th century B.C., we have to be thankful to possess such a unique work of the early centuries of our era. And whatever may be the age of the work, Indology owes a great debt or gratitude to R. Shama Śastrī who has first made the work accessible to scholars.

---

# BHĀSA

It has long been known that Bhāsa was a predecessor to Kālidāsa. In the prologue to the Mālavikāgnimitra the question is asked: "Why does the assembly pay so much honour to the work of a living poet, Kālidāsa, passing by the works of such famous poets as Bhāsa, Saumilla, Kaviputra and others?" About 200 years later the poet Bāṇa praises Bhāsa as an eminent dramatist. And again a hundred years later Vākpati, the poet of the Prākrit Epic Gauḍavaha, mentions Bhāsa among his favourite poets. Rājaśekhara (about 900 A.D.) says that in the fire of criticism the Svapnavāsavadattā alone of all the dramas of Bhāsa could not be burnt. In some of the anthologies single verses are found which are ascribed to Bhāsa. This is all that was known of Bhāsa up to the year 1910. In this year Mahāmahopādhyāya Gaṇapati Śāstrī discovered in South Travancore a palm leaf manuscript which contained ten plays and a fragment of an eleventh, one of which was called Svapnavāsavadattā and which he declared to be the lost dramas of Bhāsa. Later on he found two plays more, which showed the same peculiarities as those he had found before and which he, therefore, also declared to be works of Bhāsa. In none of these dramas, however, the name of the author is mentioned. Yet his arguments for ascribing them to the great predecessor of Kālidāsa were accepted by most Western scholars. As to Indian scholars I am not quite sure. I only know that some of them refuse to acknowledge the dramas as those of Bhāsa, while others agree with Gaṇapati Śāstrī. Which of these two parties has the majority, I do not know. Nor does it matter much. For in science truth is not found out by the majority of *votes*, but by the majority of *arguments*.

And this is certainly now one of the *great problems* of the history of Indian literature, whether the plays ascribed to Bhāsa are really his, or productions of some unknown poet and (as some scholars think) of a much later time.

But before we try to form an opinion about this problem, it will be advisable to say something about the plays themselves.

Of the thirteen plays discovered and published by Gaṇapati Śāstrī there are six short plays in which the plot is taken from the Mahābhārata, two of which treat the Rāma story, one in which the Kṛṣṇa legend forms the subject, two for which the Bṛhatkathā of Guṇādhya has supplied the plot and two which are either the poet's own invention or (what seems to me more probable) which are also taken from the Bṛhatkathā.

Five of the Mahābhārata plays (as we may call them) consist only of one act each.

In these one-act plays some short episode is taken from the Mahābhārata and very freely dramatised. There is little prose dialogue in them. They mostly consist of verses and remind us thus of their epic origin. The language is also on the whole very simple and occasionally shares some grammatical irregularities with the epic language. Yet they are all very dramatic, full of life and action. The most striking of these plays of one-act is the *Urubhanga*, the 'Breaking of the Thighs" (*viz.*, of Duryodhana). The language of the play is of great vigour and beauty. The short piece is wonderfully dramatic, and would make a great impression on the stage even to-day. And what is most remarkable it is the only tragedy in the whole of Sanskrit literature. For in violation of the rules of the Nāṭyaśāstra Duryodhana passes away— स्वर्गं गच्छति as the stage direction says on the stage.

The *Pañcarātra* is a drama in three acts, based on the Virāṭaparvan of the Mahābhārata. But a great part of the plot is freely invented by the poet. Such an invention is, that in the battle in connection with the cow raid of Duryodhana Abhimanyu, who is fighting on the side of the Kurus, is taken prisoner by Bhīma, which leads to a very dramatic scene between father and son.

The *Vālacarita* is the earliest drama preserved to us, that has the life of Kṛṣṇa for its subject. All the miraculous stories of Kṛṣṇa's childhood are known to the author such as we find them in the most modern accounts of the Kṛṣṇa legend. But there are no erotic scenes of the kind, as we find them in the Gītagovinda, nor is there any mention of Rādhā. Again we find, that the poet has with great skill taken out of the Kṛṣṇa legend everything that could be of any dramatic effect, and has invented some very dramatic scenes in addition.

In the *Vālacarita*, as well as in the *Dūtavākya* and in the *Dūtaghaṭotkaca*, Kṛṣṇa is throughout described as the Highest Being, Nārāyaṇa.

The subject of two of the 'Bhāsa-plays,' as we may provisionally call them, is the story of Rāma. The *Pratimānāṭaka* begins with the exile of Rāma and Sītā, and ends with the abduction of Sītā through Rāvaṇa. Some of the most dramatic situations are again the poet's own invention, particularly the third act, from which the play has its title. But while in the Pratimānāṭaka Rāma is only a human hero, he appears in the *Abhiṣekanāṭaka* which treats the latter part of the Rāma story as Viṣṇu-Nārāyaṇa, the only god. The first act, in which Vālin, the king of apes, dies on the stage, is a little tragedy by itself.

Compared with other Rāma dramas, for instance, those of Bhababhūti, these two plays strike us by the skill with which the poet has created the dramas, full of action, out of the epic story. The language, too, though on the whole simple enough rises sometimes to great poetical flight. Thus Laksmaṇa, when seeing the ocean breaks out into the words:

" Here, here holy Varuṇa, the lord of rivers, lies stretched out, like Hari, spreading out his thousand arms the rivers, his water, blue like sapphire, shining like a cloud, heavy with rain, the foaming waves forming his beautiful necklace."

And at the end of the 4th act the setting sun is compared to a jewel set in gold on the glowing red rug covering the temples of an elephant.

I have already mentioned that in these plays the verses far outnumber the prose passages; there is also very little Prākrit in them, and they have no comic scenes and no Vidūṣaka. With regard to all this they differ from the four 'Bhāsa-plays' belonging to the Prakaraṇa type.

The most prominent of these, no doubt the masterpiece of our poet, is the *Svapnavāsavadattā*. The plot is taken from the story of King Udayana, as it was probably told in Guṇādhya's Bṛhatkathā. We know the story from Somadeva's Kathāsaritsāgara, and the more we compare the story with the drama, the more we must admire the poet who has created the most delicate and refined drama out of a rather clumsy story.

The second of the 'Bhāsa-plays' that deals with the Udayana story is the *Pratijñāyaugandharāyaṇa*. Yet this is a drama of quite different type from the Svapnavāsavadattā; while the latter is essentially a love story, diplomacy (nīti) is the subject of the Pratijñāyaugandharāyaṇa. And the hero is the minister Yaugandharāyaṇa, a pendant to the minister Cāṇakya of the Mudrārākṣasa. Full of dramatic effect is the meeting between Yaugandharāyaṇa and the rival minister of the enemy, when the first though wounded and a prisoner, speaks proudly like a conqueror to his enemy.

The third Prakaraṇa is the *Avimāraka* which is a dramatised fairy tale, probably also taken from the Bṛhatkathā. This, too, is very dramatic and the language is sometimes very artificial, similes and long compounds proving the author to be quite familiar with the Kāvya style. The Vidūṣaka of the Avimāraka reminds us of Maitreya, the Vidūṣaka in the Mṛcchakaṭika. On the one hand he is the uneducated

Brāhmaṇa who always likes to talk of eating, but on the other hand, he is the most faithful friend of the hero.

Perhaps the most important of the 'Bhāsa-plays' is the *Daridracārudatta* or 'Cārudatta.' This is a fragment of four acts only and these four acts correspond to the first four acts of the Mṛcchakaṭika, ascribed to king Śūdraka. It may be that Cārudatta has been left incomplete by its author, and was completed and at the same time recast by Śūdraka. But it is also possible that the second part of Bhāsa's Cārudatta has been lost. But this much seems certain, that the four acts of the 'Cārudatta' we possess are older than the corresponding four acts of Mṛcchakaṭika.

The most striking difference between the 'Bhāsa-play' 'Cārudatta' and Śūdraka's Mṛcchakaṭika is this, that in the latter the love story of the merchant Cārudatta and the courtesan Vasantasenā is interwoven with a political intrigue while in the 'Bhāsa-play' there is no trace of Āryaka, the shepherd who removes the Kṣatriya Pālaka from the throne. We can see no reason why the author of the 'Cārudatta' should have carefully removed all allusions to Āryaka and Pālaka, if Śūdraka's play were the original. Besides there are a number of passages in the Mṛcchakaṭika which are clearly enlargements of the original. The investigations of Dr. Sukthankar and Dr. Morgenstiorna leave no doubt about the priority of the 'Cārudatta' to the Mṛcchakaṭika. Yet the differences between Bhāsa's Cārudatta and Sūdraka's Mṛcchakaṭika are such that we cannot call the latter a mere plagiarism. As far as we can see at present it seems that both the author of the Mṛcchakaṭika and the author of the fragment 'Cārudatta' were great poets and dramatists before the time of Kālidāsa.

But so far I have only provisionally spoken of the 'Cārudatta' and the other twelve plays as the works of Bhāsa. Now it remains for me to prove, that they are really the works of the great predecessor of Kālidāsa, or at least to state on what grounds I consider it a very probable hypothesis to see in them the dramas of Bhāsa.

For I must admit at once that as all these plays have come down to us anonymously, they cannot be ascribed to Bhāsa with absolute certainty but only with a certain degree of probability. And it will be my duty to place before you not only the arguments which speak *for* but also those which speak *against* the authorship of Bhāsa.

In order to answer the question of the authorship of these thirteen dramas, we shall have first of all to show that they all have *one* and the same author.

Now these plays have indeed much in common. They are all much shorter than all the classical plays known to us. Especially the prologue is always very short and in the prologue the author and title of the play are never mentioned as is invariably done in all the other plays of Indian literature. It may be said that these facts may also be explained by assuming that they all belong to the same school of poets or to the same part of India or to the same time. But we find also in the introductory verses (Maṅgalaśloka) of four plays (Pañcarātra, Pratimānāṭaka, Svapnavāsavadattā, and Pratijñāyaugandharāyaṇa) the same device of the Mudrālankāra (*i.e.*, allusion to the names of the principal persons of the play by means of puns). Two of the plays (Dūtavākya and Madhyama) show verbal agreements in this verse. Still more important it is that the Bharatavākya (the final benediction at the end of the play) is almost identical in several of these plays (Pañcarātra, Abhiṣeka, Svapnavāsavadattā, Pratijñāyaugandharāyaṇa, Avimāraka: imam api mahīm Kṛtsnāmrājasiṃhaḥ praśāstu naḥ "may our god-like king rule this whole earth."

These peculiarities are common to the two groups of plays, if we call the Mahābhārata plays, the Kṛṣṇa drama Vālacarita, and the two Rāma plays the first group, and the four Prakaraṇas the second group.

All the plays of the first group have this in common, that

their author must have been a strictly orthodox follower of the Brāhmaṇical religion and custom, and a zealous worshipper of Viṣṇu. He likes to introduce or to mention Brāhmaṇical rites and ceremonies, and on every possible occasion he emphasises the exalted and prominent position of the Brāhmaṇas. The Pañcarātra begins with the description of a great sacrifice, of which there is no mention in the Mahābhārata. The poet evidently invented it, in order to describe the pageant of a grand Brāhmaṇical ceremony. Here we read also such sayings as: " The sacred fire does not suffer a worldly fire by its side, as the Brāhmaṇa does not suffer a Śūdra by his side."

Or: " The king should pour his whole wealth into the lap of the Brāhmaṇa, and leave only his bow to his sons." Bhīṣma, in order to prove that he was inferior to his teacher says to Droṇa: " You are a Brāhmaṇa and I am a warrior." In the Madhyamavyāyoga Ghaṭotkaca says: "I know, everywhere and ever the Brāhmaṇas are the most venerable on earth." In the Vālacarita, the chamberlain protests against the idea that he would say an untruth, whereupon Kaṃsa appeals to him by saying: " I acknowledge even the untrue word of a Brāhmaṇa as true." Obedience to the Brāhmaṇa is the main tendency of the Karṇabhāra, which is emphasised much more than in the Mahābhārata story. In the same play Karṇa says a benediction: " Cows and Brāhmaṇas may never perish;" For sacred as the Brāhmaṇas are the cows. Thus we read also in the Pañcarātra: " Not in vain is the effort in the front of the battle for the sake of the cows, even death in such a battle will bring fame, but if one sets them free it is a religious merit." And the old herdsman in the Vālacarita opens the Hallīśa dance with the song:

" Ere the sun has risen,
Bow in veneration your heads
To the cows, the mothers of the world,
Filled with drink of immortality."

The author of these plays also likes to show his knowledge of Brāhmaṇical customs and of the Śāstra. In the Madhyama one hears a call behind the scene: *Bhostāta* "O father" and the Sūtradhāra (stage-manager) says: "No doubt, it is a Brāhmaṇa, as he says *bhoḥ*." (The Dharmasāstras teach that a Brāhmaṇa must be addressed by mentioning the name with the interjection *bhoḥ*.)

In the Dūtavākya and in the Vālacarita the poet shows himself as a devout Kṛṣṇa-worshipper in every line. In the Abhiṣekanāṭaka Rāma is throughout praised as the only God Viṣṇu or Nārāyaṇa.

In the second group of plays the Brāhmanism of the author is not so conspicuous, as in the first group, but there is nothing in them that should contradict the assumption that the author was a Brāhmaṇa and a Vaiṣṇava. In the introductory stanza of the Avimāraka Nārāyaṇa is invoked and at the beginning of the first act the king enters saying: "The sacrifices have been offered and the best Brāhmaṇas are favourably inclined to me." In the introductory verse of the Svapnavāsavadattā Balarāma the brother of Kṛṣṇa, is invoked. The scene of the first act is a hermitage, and it is full of Brāhmaṇical religiosity. A flight of cranes passing through the air is compared to the outstretched arms of Baladeva. In the beginning of the Cārudatta, we find allusions to Brāhmaṇical sacrifices. Cārudatta himself is a Brāhmaṇa wearing the sacred thread, and sends Maitreya to bring offerings to the divine Mothers. In the introductory verse of the Pratijñāyaugandharāyaṇa, it is true, Skanda, the son of Śiva, is invoked, but only in order to bring about a pun on the name of Yaugandharāyana.

It may be taken for granted that Pratijñāyaugandharāyaṇa and Svapnavāsavadattā have the same author. They not only treat episodes of the same Udayana story, but the one is presupposed by the other. In Svapnav. (VI, 18) the king says: "To be sure, thou art Yaugandharāyaṇa. By thy endeavours, feigned madness, fights and cunning schemes taught in the science of politics—I have been rescued by thee, emerging out of all troubles." At the end of the Svapnavāsavadattā a picture is shown, in which the marriage of Udayana and Vāsavadattā is represented, and we are told that the marriage ceremony was thus performed *in effigie*, as it could not be performed in reality on account of Udayana's flight. The same detail is referred to in the Pratijñāyaugandharāyaṇa. It is not found in the Kathāsaritsāgara.

The two Rāma dramas show so many literal agreements, that it cannot be doubted that they are works of the same author. In both dramas Rāma is regularly called "the Ārya," and Sītā always addresses him by "āryaputra." Bharata says (in the Pratimānāṭaka, p. 118) that ārya is the usual address in the Ikṣvāku family.

In the Dūtavākya and in the Vālacarita the weapons of Kṛṣṇa appear on the stage in a similar manner. The Madhyamavyāyoga has its title from Bhīma being called "the middlemost" (Madhyama) of the Pāṇḍava brothers. In the Pañcarātra Bhīma is called by the same name.[1] In both these plays Bhīma calls his arms his weapons.

That the plays have one author is also made probable by the fact, that certain words and phrases occur in all or several of them. I will only mention one word, which is of particular importance for the history of the Indian drama, the word *Yavanikā* which means the curtain of the theatre and also a carpet or curtain generally. Now in several of our plays this word occurs in the latter meaning. In the Pratimānāṭaka, the dying king Daśaratha swoons away at the end of the second act then we have the stage direction: Kañcukīyo yavanikāstaraṇam karoti, 'the chamberlain spreads a curtain out' (in order to cover the dead body) whereupon all the people present cry out: हाहा महाराज । हाहा महाराओ. A similar

[1] Bhīma as the second son of Kunti seems to be called the "middlemost." But among the five Pāṇḍu brothers Arjuna was really the Madhyama.

stage direction is found at the end of the Urubhaṅga, when Duryodhana has gone to heaven. In the last scene of the Svapnavāsavadattā Vāsavadattā is first recognised by the nurse behind a curtain, and then the king says: Saṃkṣipyatām yavanikā, "let the curtain be drawn up," and then only he himself sees his beloved wife again. But if anybody should doubt, whether in these cases the theatre curtains or any other curtain be meant, there can be no doubt in a highly artificial verse of the Avimāraka, where the black clouds are compared to curtains hung up in front of the host of stars (bhagaṇayavanikāḥ).

It is also worth mentioning that in such small details, as the names of persons of secondary importance several of the plays agree with one another. Vijayā is the name of the female door-keeper in the Svapnavāsavadattā, in the Prajñāyaugandharāyaṇa and again in the two Rāma dramas. And the chamberlain both of Mahāsena in the Pratijñāyaugandharāyaṇa, and of Duryodhana is called Bādarāyana.

In several of the plays we find a predilection for certain descriptions, such as is generally found in works of one and the same poet. Most remarkable is the beautiful description of the darkness of the night in the first act of the Vālacarita, in the third act of Avimāraka, and again in the first act of the Daridracārudatta. In Vālacarita and in the Daridracārudatta we find the verse which is also found in the Mṛcchakaṭika and has also been quoted by Daṇḍin in this Kāvyādarśa.

लिम्पतीव तमोऽङ्गानि वर्षतीवाञ्जनं नभः ।
असत्पुरुष सेवेव दृष्टिनिष्फलतां गता

"The darkness besmears, as it were, the body, the sky pours down as it were a rain of collyrium. Seeing has become useless like service for wicked men."

Some of the agreements between these plays are at the same time proofs of high antiquity. This applies especially to the language and above all to the *Prākṛit* of the plays. It has been proved by Dr. V. Leshy, Dr. V. S. Sukthankar and by Dr. W. Printz, that the Prākṛit in all these plays is more archaic than that of the classical plays, that it has preserved forms of the 'Old Prākṛit' which we find in the fragments of Buddhist dramas of Aśvaghoṣa and his time. As regards the Sanskrit all the plays share a number of solecisms, ungrammatical forms. Some of these are such as we also find in epic Sanskrit and this may account for their occurrence in the dramas of the first group. But we find them also, for instance, in the 'Cārudatta' where (as Dr. Sukthankar has shown) the author of the Mṛcchakaṭika has corrected them. It is true, we find solecisms also in the later writings, especially in narrative poetry. But on the whole especially when we compare the correctness of Kālidāsa's Sanskrit—I am inclined to take it as a sign of higher antiquity.

All the plays agree also with regard to the technique. They disregard the rules of the Nāṭyaśāstra in bringing scenes on the stage which would never occur in classical dramas: Duryodhana in the Urubhaṅga, Daśaratha in the Pratimānāṭaka,[1] Vālin in the Abhiṣekanāṭaka die on the stage. In Vālacarita the most violent scenes, fighting and slaying, take place on the stage. This is certainly archaic.

Another point of technique in which all the plays agree, is the rapidity in the progress of the action, for which the frequent stage direction *niṣkramya praviśya* is very characteristic. This accounts also for the shortness of all the plays, as compared with the classical dramas. Another point of agreement between all these plays is the frequent occurrence of the ākāśabhāsita, that is speaking with persons who do not actually appear on the stage, a kind of monologue, in which one person only speaks but repeats the speeches of other persons who are not on the stage, and answers them (of that kind is

[1] That Daśaratha actually dies on the stage, though it is only said, that he swoons away, is shown by the lamentations हा हा महाराज which are not heard नेपथ्ये but are spoken on the scene मञ्चे.

the Bhāṇa, which is described in the Nāṭyaśāstra, but of which we have examples only in later Sanskrit literature).

To mention only one more point of technique we find in the sixth act of the Abhiṣekanāṭaka, that the description of the battle between Rāma and Rāvaṇa is given by three Vidyādharas, each reciting one verse in turn. In the same way the sacrifice at the beginning of the Pañcarātra is described by *three* Brāhmaṇas, and in the Urubhaṅga again *three* heralds bring the news of the club fight between Bhīma and Duryodhana.

These are—it seems to me—strong reasons that make it at least highly probable, that all the thirteen plays have one and the same author. Now we have the verse of Rājaśekhara:

भासनाटकचक्रेऽपि च्छेकैः क्षिप्ते परीक्षितुम् ।
स्वप्नवासवदत्तस्य दाहकोऽभून्न पावकः ॥

which I take to mean: "when the whole series of the dramas of Bhāsa was thrown (into the fire of criticism) by the critics, to test them, the fire proved unable to burn the Svapnavāsavadattā." From this verse we may justly conclude that Rājaśekhara knew Bhāsa as the author of a great number of plays, of which Svapnavāsavadattā was most highly appreciated by the critics who found faults in all the other plays. The anecdote current among Pundits, that the plays of Bhāsa were actually subjected to a fire ordeal, in which Svapnavāsavadattā alone survived, seems to me to be invented only through a misunderstanding of Rājaśekhara's verse. At any rate, we have no reason to reject the testimony of Rājaśekhara, that Bhāsa was the author of a famous drama *Svapnavāsavadattā*. Now as Gaṇapati Śāstrī has found a collection of dramas, one of which not only has the title Svapnavāsavadattā, but is one of the finest dramas, in Indian literature worthy of the name of Bhāsa, it seems to me not too bold an hypothesis to ascribe this Svapnavāsavadattā to Bhāsa,

If Prof. L. D. Barnett says, rejecting the theory of Gaṇapati Śāstrī, that "Probably half a dozen other poets have written plays on the same theme as the Svapnavāsavadattā," I challenge him to produce even three plays on exactly the same theme and with exactly the same title. As a rule, Indian poets do not choose the same titles for their works, when treating the same subjects, as their predecessors.[1] Barnett also speaks as if dozens of poets could have created such dramas as the Svapnavāsavadattā. I doubt this very much. But if we follow Gaṇapati Śāstrī in ascribing the Svapnavāsavadattā to Bhāsa, we shall also have to accept his theory that the other 12 plays are works of the same author, as I have shown, how highly probable it is that all the plays have one and the same author. The poet *Vākpati*, the author of the Prākṛit poem *Gauḍavaha* (about 800 A.D.) calls Bhāsa Jalanamitta or "friend of the fire." The epithet would be extremely appropriate for the author of our plays. For in the *Svapnavāsavadattā* the conflagration of Lāvānaka in which Vāsavadattā was reported to have perished forms the starting point of the drama. The *Pañcarātra* begins with a vivid description of a forest fire. In the *Abhiṣekanāṭaka* Sītā enters the fire, and her chastity is testified to by Agni himself. And again in the *Avimāraka* the hero throws himself into the flames of a forest fire, but the flames are cool as sandal-wood to him, and Agni embraces him as a father his son.

I have already pointed out some features in these dramas which are archaic and make it probable that they are earlier than the dramas of Kālidāsa. Another proof of the earlier date of these plays is, I believe, also to be found in the fact, that the court life of the kings is much simpler in them, than in the plays of Kālidāsa. King Udayana always appears only

[1] I shall have to mention a second Svapnavāsavadattā presently. But it is not certain and even highly improbable that it treated the same subject. It is more likely that it was a drama on the subject of Subandhu's 'Vāsavadattā' where Kandarpaketu and Vāsavadattā fall in love after having seen each other in a dream.

in the company of his friend, the Vidūṣaka, without any retinue. There is, for instance, no mention of the Greek women, who belong to the retinue of the king in Kālidāsa's dramas.

But though there are good reasons to believe that the author of our plays is older than Kālidāsa, we dare not go too far back. It is true, the language of these plays is on the whole simpler than that of Kālidāsa. Yet we find in them also proofs enough, that their author was quite familiar with the Kāvya style, especially in the Urubhaṅga and in the Avimāraka. We even find poetical figures (Alaṅkāras) which are more frequently found in later poetry, for instance the rhyme (yamaka). Occasionally we also find learned comparisons such as in the Pañcarātra (I, 10) where (in the description of the sacrifice) it is said, that frightened by the fire five serpents came out of the holes of an anthill, just as the five senses when a person dies, come out of the holes of his body. Or in Avimāraka (V, 1) where the princess is said to shine in beauty without her ornaments like the Veda that is free of logical reasoning (vedasrutir hetu-vivarjiteva). The Mahābhārata was known to the author of the six plays in which the episodes of the epic are treated much in the form in which we have it now. In Dūtaghaṭotkaca (19) there is an allusion to the story of the Mahābhārata, that Bhīṣma of his own free will resolved to die and advised the Pāṇḍavas himself, how they could kill him. The story was certainly not part of the original Mahābhārata. The Virātaparvan also was known to the author of the Pañcarātra in the form in which we have it to-day. Rāma, as an incarnation of Viṣṇu, as he appears in the Abhiṣekanāṭaka, is not known in inscriptions of the pre-Christian time. In language and style the dramas are nearer to Kālidāsa than to Aśvaghoṣa. And as the latter most probably belongs to the second century A.D. and Kālidāsa lived in the later part of the fourth and the first half of the fifth century A.D., Bhāsa, if he is the author of our plays, can hardly be placed earlier than the end of the third or beginning of the fourth century A.D. I do not believe that he preceded Kālidāsa by more than a hundred years. To place Bhāsa before Pāṇini's time, as Gaṇapati Śāstrī does, is quite impossible. Not only are the arguments of Gaṇapati very weak, but it is impossible to assume that our dramas are separated from those of Kālidāsa by a millennium. Nor can I agree with Pundit Jayaswal and P. Chaudhuri, who have tried to make out—I am afraid with more imagination than historical facts,—that Bhāsa was the court poet of a Kāṇva King, Nārāyaṇa who ruled 53-71 B.C. It would take up too much time to show this in detail. But one of Jayaswal's arguments is, that Bhāsa knew another Mahābhārata than ours. This is certainly wrong. Where Bhāsa differs from our Mahābhārata, he has as a true dramatist changed the story freely for the sake of dramatic effect. And when Jayaswal says, that Bhāsa's language is absolutely free from the Kāvya artificialities, from alliteration, from long compounds,—all that is absolutely wrong. But also the arguments by which Sten Konow would place Bhāsa in the 2nd century A.D. are very weak. By a very weak hypothesis he places Sūdraka in the third century A.D., and by another weak hypothesis he assumes that the word Rājasiṃha in the Bharatavākya of some of our Bhāsa plays refers to a Kṣatrapa king Rudrasiṃha I, who ruled at the end of the 2nd century A.D. Two weak arguments combined do not make a strong argument. In my opinion Rājasiṃha, in these benedictions means, simply 'lion-like king' and does not refer to any particular king at all. But even if it did, there are among the Western Kṣatrapas alone three kings of the name Rudrasiṃha, one Satyasiṃha, one Siṃhasena and one Visvasiṃha, who all ruled between 180 and 388 A.D. But Siṃha as part of a king's name is so frequent at all times, that it is mere guessing, if we choose one of the other of these kings to have been the patron of Bhāsa.

However, even if we can ascribe these plays to the 3rd or 4th century A.D. as I believe, we have to be contended with, this is in itself an argument for the authorship of Bhāsa. For we know of no other great dramatist of the time between Aśvaghoṣa and Kālidāsa.

Yet it must be admitted, that we have *no direct* proofs for the authorship of Bhāsa for these plays. You will have noticed, that I only mentioned Rājaśekhara as a witness for the Svapnavāsavadattā being the work of Bhāsa. If we turn to the pages of the introduction of Gaṇapati Śāstrī to his editions of the Svapnavāsavadattā and the Pratimānāṭaka you will find many more witnesses quoted. But, unfortunately, if you begin to cross-examine these witnesses, there is always some flaw in their evidence.

Vandyaghaṭīya Sarvānanda (about 1159 A.D.) in his commentary on the Amarakoṣa, refers to Svapnavāsavādattā but without mentioning its author. Abhinavagupta, who wrote at the end of the 10th and the beginning of the 11th century, mentions in his commentary to the Bhāratīya Nātyasāśtra both Svapnavāsavadattā (fem.) and Daridracārudatta, but again without their author's name. And the same Abhinavagupta in his Dhvanyalokalocana (3, 10 ff.) quotes a verse from a drama Svapnavāsavadatta, without mentioning an author's name, but this verse is not found in our Svapnavāsavadattā and cannot be taken from it for it is quoted as an example to show, that there are poets who only care for alaṃkāras without taking any regard of rasas (sentiments). This does certainly not apply to our drama. Vāmana (about 800 A.D.) quotes three verses, which occurs in our dramas,—one in Svapnavāsavadattā (IV, 7), the other in Pratijñāyaugandharāyaṇa (IV, 3), and one in Daridracārudatta (I, 2), but unfortunately he does not mention the source, from which the verses are taken. *Daṇḍin*, a still older author on poetics, quotes the verse *limpatīva*, etc., about the darkness of the night, which is found in two of our plays, but Daṇḍin also does not mention the source from which he has taken the verse. *Bhāmaha*, another old author on poetics, older even than Daṇḍin, refers to the subject of our Pratijñāyaugandharāyaṇa, but mentions neither title nor author of the drama.

A few months before his passing away the late Jaina saint Vijaya Dharma Suri had written to me, that he had acquired a MS. of the *Nāṭyadarpaṇa* a work on dramaturgy, by *Rāmacandra* and *Guṇacandra*, the two pupils of Hemacandra. When I came to Shivpuri in Gwalior for the memorial ceremonies in honour of the saint towards the end of January of this year, I asked for this MS. and saw a copy of it. Going over the pages of this interesting work, I hit upon a quotation from 'the Svapnavāsavadattā of Bhāsa' (both title and author given: भासकृते स्वप्नवासवदत्ते). The king (Vatsarāja) says the verse quoted, while looking at the stone seat (śilātala) in the Śephālikāmaṇḍapa. The Śephālikā is mentioned in the fourth act of our play, but I was much disappointed to find, that the verse does not occur in it. In the same Nāṭyadarpaṇa a Daridracārudatta-rūpaka is mentioned without the author's name. As the Mṛcchakaṭika is also quoted, we know at least, that in the 12th century A.D. there existed both a Daridracārudatta and a Mṛcchakaṭika.

That of all the verses which are ascribed to Bhāsa in the anthologies and elsewhere not one occurs in our plays, is also fatal. It is, of course, no proof against the authorship of Bhāsa—for the verses may occur in works of Bhāsa which are lost, or they may be wrongly ascribed to the poet but at any rate it is just a cause for doubts. It is also a strange fact, that in Somadeva Puri's Yaśastilaka a verse is quoted and ascribed to the Mahākavi Bhāsa, which we actually find in the Mattavilāsaprahasana of the Pallava prince Mahendravikramavarman who ruled about 620 A.D. The verse is quoted to characterise the Śāktas of the left head :

पेया सुरा प्रियतमामुखमवीक्षितव्यं
ग्राह्यः स्वभावललितो विकृतश्च वेषः ।
येनेदमीदृशमदृश्यत मोक्षवर्त्म
दीर्घायुरस्तु भगवान् स पिनाकपाणिः ॥

This verse does not and could not occur in any of our dramas. It is possible, of course, that Somadeva has ascribed the verse to Bhāsa by mistake; it is also possible that Bhāsa has written a play, in which such a verse occurred and that Mahendravikrama cribbed it from there. But it is puzzling.

The Mattavilāsa-prahasana has been used by Barnett[1] as the basis of his hypothesis, that the anonymous plays found by Gaṇapati Śāstrī, are not the works of Bhāsa but were written by some unknown author or authors of the 7th century, the time of the Mattavilāsa. Barnett has pointed out, that this Mattavilāsa-prahasana begins in exactly the same way as the dramas ascribed to Bhāsa, namely, with the stage direction : *Nāndayante tataḥ praviśati sutradhāraḥ*, on which the Maṅgalaśloka follows. Gaṇapati Sāstrî has laid great stress on this beginning of the dramas. But I have shown that even dramas of the 10th and 12th centuries found in certain South Indian MSS., begin in the same way; I have also found the same beginning in a Malayalam MS. of the Śakuntalā drama and it is also found in a MS. of the Mudrārākṣasa.

There is in fact no essential difference between these dramas and the classical dramas, but it is merely a matter of terminology. Every performance used to begin with the Purvaraṅga, religious ceremony with music and singing, performed behind the scene and ending with the *Nāndi*, a verse in praise of some deity. The Bhāratīya-Nātyaśāstra gives such a Nāndi, which was a simple prayer in ślokas.

[1] Barnett, however, was not aware of the quotation in the Yaśastilaka.

Our classical dramas begin with a *Nāndi* which is always a verse in metre and language of the Kāvya. Then follow the words: *nāndyante sutradhāraḥ*.

Now if these MSS. which all come from the Malabar coast, begin with the words: nāndyante tataḥ praviśati sūtradhāraḥ, this only means, that the *Nāndi* which forms the end of the Purvaraṅga was sung behind the scene and that after the singing of the Nāndi the Sutradhāraḥ entered and recited the verse with which the drama begins. This verse is not considered as the Nāndi by the writers of the Malabar MSS., but simply as an introductory verse, a maṅgalaśloka while in the other MSS. this verse also is called *Nāndi* or was considered as still belonging to the *Nāndi*.

The fact, therefore, that our plays begin with the words: nāndyante, etc., can no longer be quoted as an argument for the authorship of Bhāsa. Much less can it be used as an argument for ascribing it to the age of the Mattavilāsa-prahasana (7th century A.D.). And it is an unfounded assertion of Barnett, when he says that the Mattavilāsa is similar to the 'Bhāsa plays' also in other respects. We need only look at the prologue in the Mattavilāsa in which the name of the author and the title of the play are mentioned in the usual way and which is comparatively long to see the difference. The long compounds found in the prose of the Mattavilāsa, are very rare in the Bhāsa plays. The Bharata-vākya (final benediction) also is quite different.

In his review of my book (J. R. A. S., 1923, p. 722) Dr. Barnett refers to the mention of a *Nyāyaśāstra* by *Medhātithi* which in his opinion is 'almost certainly' the Manu Bhāṣya of Medhātithi. This is, I should say, 'almost certainly wrong.' Why the Manu-bhāṣya should be called a Nyāya-śāstra, is quite unintelligible. I am in full agreement with the late Mahāmahopādhyāya Satīśchandra Vidyābhūṣaṇa who identifies the Medhātithi of Bhāsa with the Medhātithi

Gautama, mentioned in the Śāntiparvan of the Mahābhārata, in whom he sees the founder of the Anvikṣikī.[1]

Summing up, we can state the case for and against the authorship as follows:

It appears highly probable that all the thirteen plays have *one* author. This author must have been a great poet and above all a dramatic genius. Kālidāsa and Bhababhūti may be greater poets, greater masters of language than the author of these plays, but I know in the whole of Sanskrit literature no drama that could compare as a stage play with any one of the thirteen plays ascribed to Bhāsa. All the classical dramas are more or less book dramas, while these plays are one and all the works of a born dramatist, wonderfully adapted to the stage. We have it on good authority, that Bhāsa was the author of a drama with the title *Svapnavāsavadattā*. If we take out *Svapnavāsavadattā* to be the work of Bhāsa, we shall also have to adopt the hypothesis that the other twelve plays are composed by the same author. This hypothesis is further supported by archaisms in the language of the thirteen dramas, more especially in the Prākṛit, and by archaisms in the technique by which they differ from the Nātyaśāstra of Bharata. The epithet, given to Bhāsa by Vākpati, 'friend of the fire' fits very well for the author of our plays. Language and style of our dramas make it probable that they belong to the period between Aśvaghoṣa and Kālidāsa. And as Bhāsa is mentioned by Kālidāsa himself as his famous predecessor, the date that can be ascribed to the plays also supports the hypothesis that Bhāsa is their author.

But I can only speak of a *hypothesis*. For we cannot get over the facts, that the plays have come down to us *anonymously*; that Rājaśekhara is the *only certain* witness for ascribing a *Svapnavāsavadattā* to Bhāsa; that verses ascribed to Bhāsa in anthologies and elsewhere, even verses quoted from a

[1] A History of Indian Logic, Calcutta, 1921, p. 766.

Svapnavāsavadattā, are not found in our plays ; and that there are at least *some* passages in the plays, which show a highly developed *Kāvya style*.

If, in spite of all this, I still adhere to the hypothesis that Bhāsa *is* the author of these plays, the weightiest argument for me personally is this, that nearly all the plays are works of great poetical merit, worthy of the name of a Bhāsa. And let me say this : If it *should* finally be proved, that Bhāsa cannot be the author of these plays, they will yet always have to be counted among the most valuable treasures of Indian literature; and we should—even in this case—have every reason to be thankful to Mahāmahopādhyāya Gaṇapati Śāstrī, who has unearthed these treasures for us.[1]

M. WINTERNITZ

[1] Readership Lecture delivered at the Calcutta University on 16th September, 1923.